The Kurds

Also of Interest

The Gulf and the Search for Strategic Stability: Saudi Arabia, the Military Balance in the Gulf, and Trends in the Arab-Israeli Military Balance, Anthony H. Cordesman

Local Politics and Development in the Middle East, edited by Louis J. Cantori and Iliya Harik

†*Political Behavior in the Arab States,* edited by Tawfic E. Farah

†*A Concise History of the Middle East,* Second Edition, Revised and Updated, Arthur Goldschmidt, Jr.

Ataturk and the Modernization of Turkey, Jacob Landau

The Modern History of Iraq, Phebe Marr

Middle East Politics: The Military Dimension, J. C. Hurewitz

†*Religion and Politics in the Middle East,* edited by Michael Curtis

Iraq: International Relations and National Development, Edith Penrose and E. F. Penrose

PROFILES OF THE CONTEMPORARY MIDDLE EAST:

†*Syria: Modern State in an Ancient Land,* John F. Devlin

†*The Republic of Lebanon: Nation in Jeopardy,* David C. Gordon

†*Jordan: Crossroads of Middle Eastern Events,* Peter Gubser

South Yemen: A Marxist Republic in Arabia, Robert W. Stookey

Sudan, John Voll and Sarah Voll

United Arab Emirates, Malcolm Peck

†Available in hardcover and paperback.

Westview Special Studies on the Middle East

The Kurds: An Unstable Element in the Gulf
Stephen C. Pelletiere

A major—and often unpredictable—force in the Middle East for centuries, fragmented by the boundaries of Iraq, Iran, Turkey, Syria, and Russia, the Kurds remain a nation that steadfastly resists assimilation (and elimination) and that frequently engages in violent revolts. In this book, Dr. Pelletiere analyzes the factors contributing to the remarkable survival of Kurdish nationalism and places the Kurds in the context of modern Middle East history. First establishing the Kurdish identity and contrasting it with that of surrounding ethnic groups, he goes on to trace Kurdish history and to examine the configuration of the Kurdish national movement during the world wars and the period immediately following the wars, when the Kurds were temporarily supported by the Soviet Union. He also examines the Kurds' struggles against successive Middle Eastern powers and looks at the national autonomy that was forfeited because of clashes between modern and feudal forces within the Kurdish movement. The book closes with a discussion of possible future developments for the Kurds and the advantages and drawbacks of various sorts of U.S. involvement. Dr. Pelletiere destroys many myths about the Kurds and treats them not as a cultural artifact but as an important factor in the power equation of the Middle East.

Dr. Stephen Pelletiere is assistant professor of politics at Union College. He was formerly a journalist and lived with Mulla Mustafa Barzani when the legendary Kurdish leader was fighting his war against Iraq. Dr. Pelletiere has known most of the Kurdish leaders in the United States, Europe, and the Middle East and has interviewed members of the Politburo of the Kurdish Democratic party in exile in Iran.

Traditional Kurdistan Area

The Kurds:
An Unstable Element in the Gulf

Stephen C. Pelletiere

Westview Press / Boulder and London

Westview Special Studies on the Middle East

Published in 1984 in the United States of America by Westview Press, Inc., 5500 Central Avenue, Boulder, Colorado 80301; Frederick A. Praeger, President and Publisher

Library of Congress Cataloging in Publication Data
Pelletiere, Stephen C.
   The Kurds: an unstable element in the Gulf.
   (Westview special studies on the Middle East)
   Includes index.
   1. Kurds—Politics and government. 2. Near East—
Politics and government. I. Title. II. Series.
DS51.K7P44 1984   956'.0049159   83-14755
ISBN 0-89158-689-X

Printed and bound in the United States of America

5   4   3   2   1

To My Wife, Jean,
and Son, Danilo

Contents

Preface

This book examines the political significance of a Middle Eastern people, the Kurds, and it suggests that they have a great potential for making trouble. Indeed, that potential probably is greater today than at any previous time in the Kurds' long history. A number of factors contribute to this trouble-making ability. First, the Kurdish society basically is anarchic, and the Kurds have a long tradition of serving as mercenaries in the armies of Europe and the Middle East—which is to say that the Kurds are a fighting people. Second, the Kurds' traditional homeland, Kurdistan, is crucially located where the superpowers confront each other in the Gulf region. Finally, Kurdistan is an inhospitable land that is hard to penetrate, particularly with modern, mechanized armies.

Taken in combination what do these three factors tell us? The Kurds are a fighting people who would be difficult to rout, even though they are continually disrupting the peace in an area that is adjacent to the Gulf where the superpowers want to maintain stability.

Today, there is a particularly troublesome war—for the superpowers—in the Gulf. Since the summer of 1983, the principal combatants, Iran and Iraq, have been fighting each other, to a large extent through Kurdish proxies. Iran's overall war plan is to carry the fighting into Iraqi Kurdistan in the hope that the Kurds there will revolt against Baghdad. Conversely, Baghdad is subsidizing a revolt of Iranian Kurds against Tehran. This is not the first time the Kurds have become involved in a conflict that threatened to involve the world's superpowers. In fact, they have done so on three separate occasions since the end of World War I.

In this book, I offer a theory of superpower involvement in Kurdish politics. I submit that this involvement is intimate; indeed I do not believe that the frequent, violent uprisings of the Kurds can be understood except in the context of superpower penetration into the Gulf region.

I want to acknowledge the help of a number of people in the writing of this book: Frederick Praeger, for suggesting that there was a need for a book about the Kurds; George Lenczowski, for encouraging me; and two other professors of mine at Berkeley who greatly influenced me, Reinhard Bendix and Kenneth Waltz. Ralph Magnus and Phebe Marr read excerpts of the book and made many useful suggestions; and Marge Windstone and Irma Garlick prepared the manuscript. Finally, it was Arville Schaleben of the *Milwaukee Journal*, who, I believe, was one of the last great editors in American journalism, who first introduced me to the Kurds.

Stephen C. Pelletiere

1
Introduction

The Kurds have long been a subject of fascination. Books about them have been written by acting political officers in the British army, journalists, residents of the British East India Company, generals in the Iranian army (writing in English), Kurdish publicists for the Kurds, Armenian publicists for the Kurds, British officers who, having ridden overland from India to Europe, passed through Kurdistan, and secret agents (there have been many books about the Kurds by secret agents). But, with the exception of one or two fine anthropological investigations, there does not exist in English a scholarly treatment of the Kurds that covers all their various recent political involvements.

This omission is curious because the Kurds have been a significant political factor in the Middle East for centuries. Although statistics as to their actual numbers are notoriously unreliable, it still is within reason to assert that after the Arabs, Turks, and Persians, the Kurds are the most numerous of the Middle Eastern peoples. In addition, they inhabit one of the most strategic areas of the globe today: territory that separates the Soviet and Western spheres of influence in the Gulf region. And, if that were not enough, at the time of this writing the Kurds are rebelling in Iran against a government the disappearance of which could greatly complicate the strategic planning of the superpowers.

Kurdistan

For mapmakers—if not for international lawyers—there *is* such a place as Kurdistan. The Kurds inhabit a crescent of high mountains, one tip of which abuts the Euphrates in northern Syria, the other the Iranian city of Kermanshah. The bow of the crescent arches north and east (from Syria) through Turkish Armenia and Iranian Azerbaijan. Within the curve, the lowest points reached are Khanaqin (northeast of Baghdad near the Iraq-Iran border), Kirkuk, and Mosul in Iraq; and Mardin and Urfa in Turkey. Inside the crescent lies the entirety of the Zagros Mountains, a considerable portion of two great river systems—the Tigris and the Euphrates—and lesser waterways, like the Great and Little Zab rivers. No matter how the most fervent of Kurdish nationalists may construe the situation, however, at no point does Kurdistan find an outlet to any of the great seas of the region. This factor has considerably inhibited the Kurds' national development.

Kurdistan has many natural resources, although the political turmoil that has existed in Kurdish regions for over 200 years has prevented an accurate assessment of them. There are, however, two natural resources about which there can be no doubt, and both of them are precious in the Middle East: oil and water. The richest oil fields of Iraq are located around Kirkuk and Khanaqin, disputed Kurdish territory; and the rivers in Kurdish areas provide a plentiful supply of water, which can be and is being dammed and converted into electric power. Although mineral resources such as chrome and iron may exist, the area is primarily agricultural. Staple crops include wheat, barley, tobacco, rice, peas, and lentils. The Kurds also raise sheep and goats and use cattle as work animals.

The Kurds

Population

Population statistics for the Kurds cannot be trusted for the very good reason that all the countries in which the Kurds dwell have a strong vested interest in downplaying their precise numbers. Those countries are Turkey, Iran, Iraq, Syria, and the Union of Soviet Socialist Republics (USSR). At least one, Turkey, maintains the fiction—resolutely in the face of all reason—that Kurds do not exist, that what the world knows as Kurds are in fact "mountain Turks." Another country, Iraq, has written the existence of Kurds into its constitution; that is, the constitution makes reference to two "nations" in Iraq: the Arab and the Kurdish. But the Arab-dominated Iraqi government will not concede that the Kurds in Iraq are as numerous as the Iraqi Kurds claim they are. The pattern that prevails wherever the Kurds are a minority in the Middle East is that official government statistics play down their numbers.

It is important to understand how widely the estimates of Kurdish populations vary. *New York Times* reporter Dana Adams Schmidt estimates around 2 million Kurds in Iraq, 4 or 5 million in Turkey, 3 million in Iran, around 300,000 in Syria, and about 175,000 in the USSR—around 10 million all told.[1] Contributors to *People Without a Country* claim over 6 million in Turkey, over 5 million in Iran, almost 3 million in Iraq, almost 1 million in Syria, and around 200,000 in the USSR—15 million altogether.[2] Derk Kinnane, a Dutch writer and formerly a lecturer in Baghdad, puts the figures at 1.2 milliion in Iraq, 1.4 million in Iran, 2.5 million in Turkey, 250,000 in Syria, and between 20,000 and 60,000 in the USSR—a little over 5 million.[3] Even claims as to where the Kurds live vary. With the exception of ultranationalist Turks, all commentators agree that there are Kurds in Turkey, Iran, Iraq, Syria, and the USSR. But some people would also list Afghanistan; Algeria was cited to me once; and the London-based Minority Rights Group includes Lebanon.

My own estimate of the number of Kurds and their location tends to be conservative: at least 3 million in Turkey, over 2 million in Iran, close to that number in Iraq, and very small colonies in Syria and the USSR. I estimate that the total is between 7 and 7.5 million. As for their locale, they are only politically significant in Turkey, Iran, and Iraq.

Physical Attributes

The acting British high commissioner for Mesopotamia after World War I, Sir Arnold Wilson (a man who would have legislated the Kurds out of existence),[4] described the Kurds as "physically perhaps the finest specimens of the human race in the Middle East, and they resemble Afghans in character and to some extent in physiognomy."[5] Wilson is but one of many who have found the Kurds to be physically impressive. André Singer, an anthropologist, speaks of them as "practically the only Central Asian group that remained unmixed by the influx of invading nations." He notes that although invading Mongols, Arabs, Persians, Turks, and even Macedonians all left their mark on other indigenous peoples, the Kurds in their protected mountainous home were able to preserve their identity.[6]

Character

Assessments of the Kurds' character also tend to be romanticized. Ely Soane quotes a traditional opinion in the Middle East about Kurds:

> Shedders of blood, raisers of strife, seekers after turmoil and uproar, robbers and brigands; a people all malignant and evil-doers of depraved habits, ignorant of all mercy, devoid of all humanity, scorning the garment of wisdom; but a brave race and fearless, of a hospitality grateful to the soul, in truth and honor unequalled, of pleasing countenance and fair cheek, boasting all the goods of beauty and grace.[7]

The exaggerated character assessments and admiration of the Kurds as physical specimens may be accounted for—at least in part—by the contrast between the Kurds and other Middle Eastern peoples encountered by early travelers.

The Kurds differed in three obvious respects from their neighbors. First, they were a mountain people and more often than not, free. Kurdish women did not wear the veil, and they worked alongside the men—which to a Western traveler would have seemed preferable to the seclusion in which Arab, Turkish, and Persian women are kept. Second, the Kurds were exuberant and flamboyant, characteristics embodied in their splendid costumes. To this day, Kurdish men and women favor floral scarves and cummerbunds, and the women drape themselves with chains of gold coins. Third, and an attribute the British travelers, themselves gentry, particularly admired, the Kurds were superb—but by all accounts reckless—horsemen. In fact, it was as mounted cavalry that the Kurds achieved notoriety, much like the Cossacks. In the early 1800s, when the czars went to war against Persia, two-thirds of the Persian forces were made up of Kurdish tribesmen.[8]

Society

Today, in the more primitive areas such as northeastern Iraq, the tribe is the natural unit of allegiance, and there is communal distribution of wealth. However, in most parts of Kurdistan, the land is owned by wealthy *agha*s, descendants of Kurdish lords who, in earlier times, held the land in fief. Originally, the Kurds were nomads, but at the beginning of the sixteenth century, under Sultan Selim I, the nomadic way of life came under attack by the Ottomans who needed Kurdish tribesmen as border guards. Hence, the Turks imposed the feudal pattern on Kurdistan, an important point to remember even though feudalism died out in Kurdistan at the end of the nineteenth century.[9] The Kurds' refractoriness, which gives so much trouble to governments of the Middle East today, is probably an inherited trait. The Turks encouraged the Kurds to be wild, even savage, so they would frighten off the encroaching Persians to the East.

There was a contradictory element in Kurdish character. Along with their fierce independence, the tribesmen obeyed their leaders without question, and these leaders exercised the power of life and death over the tribesmen. Such control is a feature of nomadism since a tribe that is constantly on the move with all of its worldly possessions is vulnerable to predators. Hence, the nomadic tribe must allow itself to be organized and must follow the orders of its leaders.

By the nineteenth century, although there were few purely nomadic tribes left among the Kurds, the largest of them—the Jaf and the Herki—were formidable aggregations. In 1820, the Jaf tribe totaled 60,000 and was wholly nomadic until 1900. However, in the 1950s, only 2,000 to 3,000 of the Jaf tribesmen were still nomads,[10] and by the time the Kurds become of interest to us (that is, in comparatively recent modern times), not only had nomadism all but disappeared, but the institution of the freeholding tribesman had also declined. The pattern has been to move from nomadism to feudalism to landlordism—the last I equate with detribalization. Under the British, the *agha*s were easily induced to fall in line with British-sponsored proposals to register tribal land in their names, which encouraged a trend toward private property relations started by the Turks. The essence of tribalism is that a tribe owns its land in common; landlordism is the antithesis of that principle.

Tribal organization persists in the more primitive regions of Kurdistan up to the present day. One can still find Kurds who owe allegiance to no man, manufacture their own clothes, and raise food on their own land. Commodity exchange is almost unknown to these primitive people, of whom Barzani, the great Kurdish guerrilla leader I will have occasion to refer to later, was one.

As market relations replaced feudal relations in Turkey, Iraq, and Iran, detribalized Kurds were driven, or drifted, off the land to the major cities of the Middle East where they became unskilled laborers, so that today, whole quarters are given over to Kurds in Beirut and Damascus. These expatriates have been de-Kurdified and have identified with the dominant cultural group. Some have risen very high—as Syrians (for example, Husni Zaim and Khalid Bokdosh), Turks (Ismet Inonu), or Iraqis (Abdul Karim Kassem)—but these people are exceptional, since the path to the top for Kurds, even when they assimilate, is generally difficult.

Mostly the Kurds are illiterate. Ismet Vanly, writing in *People Without a Country,* says that in 1971, Irbil (Iraq), the richest of the Kurdish provinces, had only seventy school-children per 1,000 inhabitants.[11] The Kurds are also poor. In Turkey they are the principal denizens of the shantytowns that pustulate around the major industrialized cities.

Discrimination

The Kurds are woefully discriminated against on three grounds: race, religion, and history. Racially they are distinct. They are Aryans, like the Iranians, and the language they speak is of the Indo-European group, which sets them apart from the Semitic-speaking Arabs in Iraq and Turkic speakers in Turkey. But even though they are linguistically allied with the Iranians, the two languages are not mutually intelligible.

In regard to religion, the Kurds and Iranians are also different. By and large, Kurds are Sunni Muslims. In Iran, where the state religion is Shiism, Kurds who might ordinarily live as equals with their racial brothers are alienated on the grounds of religion. And, ironically, in Iraq the situation is precisely the reverse. There the Kurds are coreligionists of the dominant Sunni Arabs, but as Kurds (that is, non-Arabs) they are considered aliens.

Finally, the Kurds are discriminated against because of their alleged past wrongs. The Middle East is an area racked by ancient feuds, and as neighbors of the Turks, Persians, Arabs, Armenians, Assyrians, and Jews, the Kurds have meted out their share of punishment over the centuries. In the way of things in the Middle East, such acts must be repaid.

The Ancient History of the Kurds

The earliest known significant record (that is, one that would have meaning for a layman) that refers to a people who might have been Kurds is Xenophon's *Anabasis*. When 10,000 Greeks retreated from Persia after the Persian prince they served was treacherously murdered (401–400 B.C.), they passed through the Zagros Mountains where they encountered the Karduchoi. These savage people rolled boulders down upon the retreating Greeks, smashing one man's leg.[12] This incident is widely quoted, and the claim is made that the Karduchoi were Kurds. However, Minorsky writes: "There is nothing really surprising in finding at the time of Xenophon an Iranian tribe settled to the north of the Tigris, but we have nothing but the evidence of the name from which to judge the ethnology of the Karduchoi."[13] Minorsky then goes on to show how the name might better be construed as Assyrian, that is, Semitic.

The same situation applies to much of the early historical evidence. The link (usually a philological one) is interesting—that is, the name suggests a link between some ancient people and today's Kurds—but in the earliest records there is not one scrap of evidence that is conclusive. For example, there are ancient inscriptions bearing reference to a country Karda-ka (Sumerian) in the year 2,000 B.C. and to another, Kurti-e, a thousand years later. However, these are bare inscriptions, nothing more. The Kurds themselves believe that they are the sons of the Medes (seventh and sixth centuries B.C.), and, indeed, the marching song (or national anthem) of the Kurdish guerrillas goes, "We are the sons of Medes and Kay Kusraow / Our God is Kurdistan."[14] This link is based upon cuneiform records of a people, the Guta (which means "warrior"), and the word is rendered in Assyrian by the synonym *gardu* or *kardu*. After the fall of the ancient city of Nineveh, these people coalesced with the Medes and became Aryanized.[15]

Thus scholars are on unsure ground when trying to establish definitely the early origins of the Kurds. There are two favored hypotheses: Either the Kurdish people spring from Iranian tribes that immigrated into the Zagros Mountains in prehistoric times and established themselves there, or these Iranian tribes, migrating west, imposed themselves on an autochthonous people and have exploited them ever since. The Kurds themselves favor the former interpretation, explaining that whatever differences there are between the body types of the fighting tribesmen and the peasants, called *miskin,* are the result of differences in diet. Defenders of the second hypothesis point out that the body types are too disparate. In any event, it is certain that the conventional wisdom about the Kurds—that they are all uniformly handsome, tall, and aquiline—is nonsense. As Minorsky writes, one has only to look at the photographs in Sir Mark Sykes *The Caliph's Last Heritage* (London: Macmillan, 1915) to see the difference between the types of Kurds: the Milli (Arab type), Girdi (Mukri type), Shamdinan (Nestorian and Hakkari types) and Kockiri (biblical Jew type).

Beginning with the Arab conquest, our knowledge about the Kurds becomes sure. Arab historians of the Muslim period (Masudi, about A.D. 943) preserved traditions from the pre-Islamic period of feuds between the Arab princes of Ghassān and the Kurds, but the first contact between Muslims and Kurds came after the occupation of Tikrit and Hulwan north of Baghdad, in A.D. 637. There are records of Arabs fighting Kurds who had taken up the cause of al-Hurmuzan, the Persian governor of Ahwaz in present Khuzestan (Iran), and ultimately, Caliph Omar had to send several expeditions against the Kurds of Ahwaz. Nor was the nearby Kurdish area of Shahrizur subjugated without bloody fighting. It was not unusual for the Kurds, once subdued, to rise again and have to be reconquered many times. Nevertheless, until very recent times, the Kurds prided themselves on their intermingling with the Arabs, and it became a patent of nobility to be able to trace one's ancestry to one of Mohammad's captains.

Prior to the Arab conquest, the Kurds probably were Zoroastrians (Noo Ruz, the Kurd's national holiday, is a fire-worshiping celebration), although some commentators claim that they were pagans who worshiped trees and sacrificed to an idol of copper. The Kurds submitted to Islam, although in some cases they had to be forced to do so. There were also incidences of apostasy; for instance, Kurds at Berudh, near Basrah in southern Iraq, who had been forcibly converted later renounced Islam en masse. In fact, it is hard to say how deeply the new religion of Islam affected the Kurds (today, they are prone to extremist practices). Hanna Batatu claims that in Iraq the three major variants of Islam are Sunnism and Shiism among the Arabs and Sufism among the Kurds.[16]

Nevertheless, the Kurds can claim to have produced the greatest champion of Islam, Salahadin. This great Muslim warrior, who defeated Richard the Lion-Heart in 1192, was a Kurd of the Ayubi dynasty and was originally based in Tikrit. Salahadin accomplished the feat of joining the kingdoms of Egypt, Syria, and Iraq, and by means of this invincible combination, he defeated the Crusaders, driving them out of Jerusalem and reducing their holdings to a handful of castles on the Syrian littoral. Kurdish nationalists criticize Salahadin for not creating a Kurdish empire, but not only did he fail to do that, he never subdued Kurdistan; his empire ended at the foothills of the Zagros chain. The Kurds served him, but in many cases they did so grudgingly, and Kurdish chiefs even disputed his right to assume the leadership of the Ayubi dynasty.

The erratic nature of the Kurds is marked in all periods of Islam. They would fight for the faith, but it was not safe to count on them. This was not the case with the Mongol invasion of the thirteenth century, however. The Kurds have a fairly consistent record of opposing the Il-khans—one reason being the Mongols favored the Christians—so the Kurds had a common cause with the Mamaluk sultans who ultimately defeated the Mongols.

After the Mongols, several Turkoman dynasties extended their power over Kurdistan. The famous Tatar warrior Timur had to deal with the Kurds in his campaign of A.D. 1400–1401, and after overrunning Baghdad, he attacked the Kurds to the north in Jazira Ibn Omar, the region between Lake Van and Lake Urmia in the north and Mosul and Rawanduz in the south. However, Timur did befriend the Kurdish chief at Bitlis in Turkey, a man who was renowned for his justice. After the death of Timur, the Kurds had to confront various Turkoman tribes, particularly the Ak-Konyunlu (the Bayandur dynasty), which made it a systematic policy to exterminate the Kurds. In summary, the Kurds fared badly under both the Mongols and the Turkomans.

The modern history of the Kurds dates from the establishment of the Ottoman Empire in the sixteenth century and the clash between the Ottomans and the Persian Safavids. For three hundred years, down to the beginning of the nineteenth century, the Kurds shrewdly manipulated the balance of power between these two empires so as to preserve their petty principalities under practically independent Kurdish dynasties. These dynasties are the glorious remembrance of present-day Kurdish nationalists.

The Kurds and the International Balance

It is my belief that the Kurds are a significant people today but for reasons that are not generally appreciated. It is necessary therefore to interject a little theory here.

Kenneth Waltz argues that in today's bipolar world it may be profitable to think of the two major superpowers as system managers.[17] Rather than desiring the absolute elimination of the other, each superpower may see its role as managing its separate sphere of interest and within that sphere, arranging matters to keep the peace generally. The Gulf thus assumes extreme importance because it is one of the few areas of today's world in which the spheres of the two superpowers overlap. To the north of the Gulf are the Russian oil fields of Baku, the West's major source of oil is in the Gulf region, and just north of the Gulf, stretching from Sinkiang to Turkey, is the USSR's vulnerable underbelly. From a strategic and economic angle, neither the USSR nor the West can afford dangerous adventures in this region. Instead, both have shown a preference for dealing, not with the revolutionists of the area, but with the established governments. It is my thesis that imperial control over the Gulf region—whether exercised by the United States and the Soviet Union in this century or by Britain and Russia in the last—aims at preserving stability there and that it is when one or more of the imperial powers turn their attention from the Gulf that the Kurdish tribes erupt. I shall develop this argument further in later chapters.

Now let us consider the deteriorating condition of the region within the past few years. The most advanced stage of dissolution has been reached in Iran, where stable government has all but disappeared under the rule of the fundamentalist mullahs. The situation in Iran's neighboring state of Turkey is equally marked. At present, martial law is in force there; formerly, there was undeclared civil war. And Iraq, which appeared to have its internal opposition under control in 1975, is none too stable now because of its war with Iran. In all these countries the Kurds pose a significant threat. The Kurds of Turkey and Iraq showed in the not too distant past that they were disposed to fight the central government; the Kurds of Iran are doing so now.

Therefore, in one of the most crucial areas of the world where the superpowers desire stability above all else, there is a persistent anarchy that might be described as centering around a "free Kurdistan." The Kurds' significance, then, is that they represent an ingrained tendency toward disruption, toward resistance to central authority, toward going one's own way. And as such—an aggravating, unmanageable social force—they pose a worrisome problem for the system managers, the United States and the USSR.

The Kurdish National Movement

Nationalism is a method whereby consciousness is raised—a consciousness of a people's political identity, of their very existence. The belief on the part of a mass of people that they are distinctive, set off from their fellows, and by virtue of their distinctiveness entitled *by right* to a state of their own is not something that arises spontaneously or that individuals are born with. People assign their primary loyalty to a tribe or a village or a sect quite naturally. The appeal of nationalism is based on a more mature awareness, and it proceeds from the recognition that a unit of protection greater than any tribe or village or sect is an absolute necessity. In other words, the development of a sense of nationhood is preliminary to building an intimidating war machine. Nationalism is used to mobilize a people to conquer and to turn the vanquished into toilers so the war machine may further extend conquests.

The Kurds have never been aggressively nationalistic. For them, the effective unit of allegiance has remained the tribe. A tribe is a community, or a confederation of communities, that exists for the protection of its members against external aggression and for the maintenance of the old customs and standard of living. In many parts of the world the tribe has died out, but it has persisted in Kurdistan because of the peculiar terrain of that region. Locked within their respective mountain valleys, the Kurdish tribes, with their extraordinary internal cohesion (secured by endogamous marriages), successfully resisted waves of foreign invaders. But in fairly recent times, the tribal system has been largely undermined by a penetration into Kurdistan, not of men but of the concept of private property. The British and the Turks before them made it possible for tribal chiefs to take legal possession of land that formerly was communally owned, which meant that freeholding tribesmen became tenants. Later on, many of these tenants were driven off the land.

Thus, by the early part of the twentieth century—when the whole Kurdish society came under assault by the Turks, later by the Arabs, and to a certain degree by the Iranians—the society was already in disarray. To withstand the assaults upon it, the Kurds needed a mobilizing idea, and this was what Kurdish nationalism was meant to be. But until recently, Kurdish nationalism was the passion of only a few city-bred intellectuals, and it had no roots in the economic, political, or psychological life of the countryside.[18] This situation proved a confounding problem because Kurdish society is largely agricultural.

It is the tribal sector that has provided the fighters in every uprising of the Kurds against central authority. These rural, tribal elements are led by their *agha*s, who are always ready for a confrontation with authority. But they are also notorious for calling off the fighting tribesmen before any concrete results are achieved. The *agha*s will associate themselves with a movement just long enough to realize some personal gain— then they decamp with their followers.[19]

By the late 1940s, and certainly by the time of Mulla Mustafa Barzani's spectacular revolt in northern Iraq in the 1960s, a beginning had been made toward bridging the gap between the city leaders and tribal fighters. Barzani seemed to appreciate that twentieth-century Kurds could not go on in the old way. Although a tribalist himself, he had seen something of the world as an exile in the Soviet Union. Barzani was the first tribal leader the Kurdish intellectuals were able to work with, and in the revolt of the 1960s, members of the Kurdish Democratic party (KDP), a purely urban phenomenon, fought alongside Barzani in the mountains of the north. But although the KDP and Barzani's followers persisted in alliance for a time, that cooperation was not sustained. In 1964, the KDP and the Kurdish tribes loyal to Barzani fell out over a matter of policy, and Barzani drove the KDP leaders into exile in Iran. It was at this time that my intimate connection with the Kurds and their movement began.

In the autumn of 1964, I went as a journalist to interview Barzani during a lull in the Kurdish-Iraqi war, which was then three years old.[20] In Iran, as a result of a fortunate coincidence, I met the leader of the KDP while they were "guests" of the shah and living in a hotel on the outskirts of Tehran. I had several conversations with them over a period of days before crossing the Iran-Iraq border at Marivan and proceeding north to Barzani's headquarters in Raniyah. I interviewed him there, and in moving around the rebel-controlled region I also had an opportunity to observe the Kurdish nationalist movement in action.

Since my visit, I have had ample time to sift through my experiences in the Kurdish mountains and to reflect on my conversations with Barzani and the KDP leaders. I have concluded that in 1964, the Kurdish movement was on the point of surpassing itself. It was ready to develop into a real war of national liberation, but it was thwarted—blocked by a failure of leadership, on both Barzani's part and that of the KDP. The leaders simply did not have the breadth of understanding necessary to put together a movement that could endure.

By 1964, the Kurdish national movement had achieved three of the four essential requirements of a legitimate popular movement of national liberation.[21] First of all, a national movement, to be serious, must retain the capability of denying access to a specific portion of territory. The area need not be large; for instance, in the case of the Palestinian national movement in its early, formative period the territory was only the refugee camps in Jordan and later in Lebanon. In the case of the Kurdish national movement in 1964 the rebels had seized and were holding the northeastern corner of Iraq and were denying access to the Baghdad government.

The second absolute requirement of a serious movement is that of control: A movement's leaders must exercise authority over the area in which they operate. In Iraqi Kurdistan when I was there, the Kurdish leaders functioned as judges, administrators, tax collectors, and minions of the law in meting out punishment. Thus, in terms the Middle East understands, these leaders retained the power "to bind and loose."

The third requisite is the assumption of a correct adversary position. In any movement that aims at a radical power realignment, the leaders must establish beyond doubt in whose interests they operate. In other words, they must put themselves on record as advocating system-threatening stands. In 1964, the Kurdish leaders had taken such an unequivocal position.

In asking for an autonomous region of Kurdistan they were asking to share power with the Arab rulers in Baghdad.

But the reason the movement failed was that it did not achieve the fourth, and perhaps the most essential, requirement of all: It never succeeded in mobilizing the human potential of the Kurdish people. That is to say, the movement never became truly popular. Until very late in the rebellion, the brunt of the fighting was borne by Barzani's followers and the tribes associated with them. Large numbers of city Kurds associated themselves with the revolt only when driven to do so by the persecutions by the Arabs in Baghdad. When—as happened in 1964 and again in 1973—the urban Kurds were forced into the mountains by the Arabs, the movement could not accommodate them in its command structure.

In 1964, the KDP tried to become the kind of party that functions to mobilize the masses. But Barzani correctly foresaw that ultimately, the ambitions of the KDP would lead to a form of collective leadership in which the urban Kurdish elements could share, and he could not accommodate himself to any such change. Until the movement collapsed in 1975, Barzani remained its sole leader.

My overall assessment of the Kurdish national movement up to 1975 is that it labored under two major constraints. First, geopolitics worked against it as the movement could not succeed if the superpowers set themselves against it. The Kurdish region is too vital for either the USSR or the United States to countenance insurrection there, and as long as a movement is viewed as potentially destabilizing, the great powers will work against it.

Second, the movement was inhibited internally. The Kurds have never resolved one outstanding contradiction; that is, the tribesmen, who bear the brunt of the fighting, are the least amenable to politicization. A politicized, disciplined movement could reasonably be expected to stand up to pressure from even the superpowers (certainly the Zionist movement has succeeded in that respect), and it could conceivably get around the intractability of the tribesmen by directing its mobilization appeal to the detribalized elements, which represent the full revolutionary potential of the movement. To date, the Kurdish national movement has failed to entice significant numbers of recruits from this large pool.

2
Detribalization and Anarchy and Expansion

In the modern history of the Kurds there have been two significant and more or less coincidental developments: first, the deterioration of feudalism and the consequent process of detribalization and second, the remarkable growth of the Kurds both in number and in area.

The Era of Detribalization

During the reign of Sultan Selim I (ca. 1465–1520), the Turks introduced a policy of dividing the eastern region of Anatolia into military fiefs, thus establishing feudalism. Chiefs of varied origins ruled over the Kurds (and Kurdicized and Christian tribes) with the aid of some warlike Kurdish tribes.

The feudal system gradually deteriorated until, when the Turks introduced the concept of private property in the second half of the nineteenth century, it all but disappeared. By the beginning of the twentieth century, the function of the Kurdish chiefs had changed. They had become simple landlords—large landholders in many cases but no longer the patriarchs of old—and detribalization resulted.

Feudalism Under the Turks

The social order of the areas of the Middle East controlled by the Turks was feudal, but the Turkish style of feudalism should not be confused with that in the West. Under the Turks there was little or no private property, and land fell into one of three categories: state land *(mamleket* or *miri),* which included most of the land; land belonging to religious establishments *(waqf);* and true private land *(mulk),* of which there was a comparatively insignificant amount concentrated in the larger cities.[1]

The state lands were allocated to loyal knights, called *sipahis,* who were charged with providing horse and foot troops when the Turks demanded them.[2] The tribes that had previously occupied the land were not evicted; they were placed under the jurisdiction of the knights. The Turks controlled the knights by subtle and devious means, which were effective even over the great Kurdish family of Baban, which, in the latter part of the eighteenth and the early nineteenth century, controlled most of present-day Iraqi Kurdistan.

The Turkish Method of Imperial Control. The standard Turkish procedure in dealing with potentially refractory vassals was to sow discord. The Babans, members of a large family with many contentious collateral lines, were continually beset by factionalism. The Turks played relatives off against each other—holding out the prize of the *pashalik,* an honorary title that also conferred possession of land. Since there was little private ownership of property, removal of the *pashalik*—after it had been transferred to one of one's many relatives—meant a serious loss.

There was a saying current in the early 1800s: "The jealousies of the Kurdish princes are their ruin." Claudius Rich, a resident of the East India Company in Baghdad who toured Iraq at the beginning of the nineteenth century, was told by a Baban prince that "neither the Persians nor the Turks would ever be able to do anything against us [meaning the Babans] but by availing themselves of our divisions and the family jealousies of our chiefs."[3]

This explanation of the Kurds' subjugation may appear too pat unless one understands the subtlety of the Turks' method. They set one tribe against another, one family member against his kin, but they never permitted any tribe or family member, with his retainers, to be utterly wiped out. Instead, they preserved the victim, intending to raise him up again at a later date.[4]

Abdur Rahman Baban. An example of the Turkish method of administering the empire is the treatment of Abdur Rahman Baban. In the first decade of the nineteenth century, the Turkish governor of Baghdad acted to bring the independent Baban principality under his control, and thus began the decline of the outstanding autonomous chieftainship of Kurdistan.

Abdur Rahman was perhaps the last of the great Babans. By constantly intriguing with and against the Turkish governor in Baghdad and the Persians across the frontier, he managed to seize and hold the city of as-Sulaymaniyah, capital of the *pashalik* of Shahrizur, no fewer than three times.[5] In 1813, he was finally deposed and died a natural death.

Abdur Rahman's ambitions have been variously interpreted, and some people make him out to be a liberator. Mrs. Rich, who kept a journal when she accompanied her husband on his Kurdistan tour, quotes an edifying speech supposedly spoken by Abdur Rahman in Derbend, which lay between as-Sulaymaniyah and Baghdad, where he was twice defeated (the first time in 1805). He is supposed to have torn his beard, wept, and foamed at the mouth with rage and disappointment, exclaiming, "While I am doing my utmost to liberate my country, one of my own family betrays it!"[6] (Abdur Rahman's flank was turned by the Turks as a result of treachery on the part of a Kurd hostile to the chief's cause.) Claudius Rich, himself, was taken by Abdur Rahman, and Rich describes him as an old friend.[7] Stephen Longrigg, on the other hand, regards him as something of a pirate.[8]

The bare facts of his career are presented in Stephen Longrigg's book.[9] Abdur Rahman took over the *pashalik* of Shahrizur (roughly the area bounded by the Little Zab River on the north, the province of Baghdad on the west, that of Diyalah on the south, and the Persian frontier on the east) in 1789. In 1792, and again in 1794 and 1799, he supplied forces to the governor of Baghdad, his overlord. Then he was deposed, apparently in keeping with the Turkish policy of promoting division among the Babans, and his cousin replaced him. In 1802, he was held captive by the Baghdad governor, but he regained control of his pashalik in the same year and again loyally assisted his overlord. But his loyalty did not last: In 1805, he revolted and defeated the army sent by the Turks to subdue him. He then retired to a previously prepared fortress at Derbend, but as in 1808, he was driven off, and his throne was given to a kinsman, Khalid.

Abdur Rahman then fled to the Persians, who supported him readily. The shah requested his reinstatement, knowing that the certain refusal, which was not long in coming, would give the Persians an excuse to invade. This collusion was the first of a long series of intrigues between Abdur Rahman and the shah, and in this case it was successful. The Turks were overcome, and Abdur Rahman regained control of as-Sulaymaniyah. He seized Koi Sanjak north of Kirkuk, but he was again confined at Derbend, and again his position was compromised. In fact, the whole drama was repeated. With the Persians once more supporting him, he was again reinstated, but then he fell afoul of both sides, Baghdad and the shah. He was deposed again in 1811, and in 1812, he was finally defeated. After that, the Baban kingdom rapidly declined.

A long struggle between two brothers, both claimants to Abdur Rahman's throne, weakened the family irreparably.[10] The region became more and more dominated by Persia, and a Persian garrison remained in as-Sulaymaniyah until the death of Fath Ali Shah in 1834.[11] The Babans' northern neighbor then started to gain ground under its chief, Kor Mohammad of Rawanduz.[12] The Babans hung on, but the family was already in eclipse when the great revolts of the post-1826 period broke out. There was a brief recrudescence under Ahmad Baban in the late 1840s, when the family put together a fighting force modeled on the *nizam jadid*,[13] but by 1851, the last Baban had been replaced by a Turkish governor.

Daud Pasha. The Turkish method of imperial control was ingenious, but its success depended on a particularly shrewd and arbitrary governor being set over the lesser pashas, such as the Kurdish chiefs. This regional overlord, if he was any good at all, was more than likely to want to aggrandize himself to the point at which it would be problematic whether Constantinople could control him. Such a one was Daud, the governor of Baghdad, who administered the region of Kurdistan at the beginning of the nineteenth century.

At this time, a four-way struggle for power had commenced in the Turkish-Persian-Mesopotamian triangle in southeastern Anatolia and western Persia. Baghdad was ruled by a dynasty made up of Georgian ex-slaves, the Kulemenis, who formed a military order similar to the Ottoman Janissaries and the Egyptian Mamalukes. The last of the Kulemenis line, Daud Pasha, was active in attempts to centralize control over all of what is now Iraq. He suppressed tribal revolts, dismissed shaikhs and *agha*s who would not, or could not, serve him, and placed his own people as heads of the tribes.

The Kulemenis nominally were vassals of the Grand Turk, but—as with so many similar arrangements in those days in that part of the world—this allegiance was honored more in the breach than otherwise. In the first decade of the nineteenth century, the immediate opposition to the Georgians was the Kurds, particularly the Baban pashas of as-Sulaymaniyah, who had allied themselves with the Persians.

To break up this combination, Daud took to the field with his army in 1821—and was defeated. Daud retaliated against Persians living in Iraq, and this action brought on the Turco-Iranian war of 1821–1823. With an army partially reorganized along European lines and assisted by the Kurds, the Persians attacked both in the north, penetrating as far as Bitlis, and in the south toward as-Sulaymaniyah. The Persian army was successful but decimated by cholera, which forced the Persians to agree to the Erzurum Peace Treaty (March 1823), according to which Iraqi Kurdistan was to remain in the hands of the Turkish state. The Persians then retreated behind the Zagros

Mountains and did not seriously assert claims beyond that range again. In 1831, Daud Pasha was deposed by the Turks, who, by that time, had made up their minds to incorporate Iraq into the administrative system of the empire. Thus they meant to bring Turkish Kurdistan, including as-Sulaymaniyah, the *pashalik* of the Babans, under their direct jurisdiction.

Nizam Jadid

The ambition of the Turks after 1826 was not simply to repossess Iraq—indeed, Iraq in its sorry conditon was hardly a prize. The Turks had a much more ambitious scheme, for the successful achievement of which control of Iraq was a prerequisite.

When the Turkish military machine was in good running order it was marvelously effective, but by the seventeenth century it had begun to run down. Lutsky writes that at one time, the sultan had been able to recruit 100,000 to 120,000 vassals to fight, but in the seventeenth century only 7,000 or 8,000 went on campaigns.[14]

From the eighteenth century onward, Russia began crowding the Turks in its push southward for warm-water ports, and the Russian army was better equipped—primarily with fire-arms—than the Turkish forces. In the early nineteenth century, Turkish soldiers were still using swords and bows and arrows, and the Kurds, who were among the auxiliaries of the Turks, were no better equipped. In the 1911 edition of the *Encyclopaedia Britannica* one can find this description of the Kurds:

> There was up to a recent period no more picturesque or interesting scene to be witnessed in the east than the court of one of these great Kurdish chiefs where, like another Saladin, the bey ruled in patriarchal state, surrounded by an hereditary nobility, regarded by his clansmen with reverence and affection and attended by a bodyguard of young Kurdish warriors clad in chain armour, with flaunting silken scarves, and bearing lance and sword as in the time of the crusades.[15]

It was at least partly because the Turks depended on such ill-equipped forces that they were continually being forced to give ground to the Russians. Therefore, in 1826, Sultan Mahmud II and the Turks set out to effect a complete overhaul of their fighting machine. This effort was the famous *nizam jadid,* or "new order." To raise money for the "new army" (modeled on the most up-to-date European lines), the Turks had to devise a way to achieve a more thorough collection of taxes. They also required infantrymen, for the reconstituted force depended on foot-soldiers, not cavalry—which is what the Kurds primarily supplied. The Turks' task was therefore twofold. They first had to subdue Iraq (which they planned to do by eliminating those chiefs—like the Babans—who had elevated themselves into the position of being petty princes), and they then had to bind the Iraqis (both Arabs and Kurds) to the land so they could be easily recruited when necessary and made to pay taxes.

The full onslaught of the Turks' consciously pursued policy to smash the tribes began in 1826 and was effected in two stages. The first was a phase of ruthlessness during which the Turks applied fire and sword; the second phase, the introduction of private property ownership, was more guileful.

The Phase of Fire and Sword. The principal Kurdish rebellions of this period of Turkish ruthlessness were those of Kor Mohammad in 1826 and Prince Badr Khan in 1847. About 1826, Kor Mohammad, the Kurdish chief of Rawanduz, declared himself independent and attacked the Khoshnaw tribe.[16] In 1831, he seized Irbil, Altun-Kupri, Koi Sanjak, and Raniyah, and the following year he took Mosul, Akra, Zibar, and al-Amadiyah in northern Iraq. By 1833, he had taken territory up to Zakho and Jazira on the present Turkish border. And then, almost as suddenly as the rebellion had begun, it collapsed.[17] In 1835, Turkish troops under a pasha, Rashid, sent from Constantinople appeared at Diyarbakir. Rashid pacified Mardin and, in the process, permanently detached that area from Mosul to Diyarbakir. Then, joined by the governor of Baghdad, Ali Rida, Rashid proceeded against

Mohammad with a formidable host. The latter's army began to melt away, and in 1836, Mohammad was captured by means of a ruse. He was sent to Baghdad where he was murdered.

Various explanations are offered for the sudden collapse of Mohammad's rebellion. Longrigg refers to the chief's "impeccable discipline" maintained by his "just severity,"[18] He apparently maintained order in the vast stretch of territory he seized—at one point, he controlled an area from Baghdad to today's Iraq-Iran and Iraq-Syria border—but he excited neither gratitude nor loyalty in his subjects. Another version is that the Turks simply bought off Kor Mohammad's allies,[19] which—if true—is a clear indication of the condition of Kurdish national consciousness at the time. After the destruction of Kor Mohammad, Kurdistan erupted in violence, and the next significant uprising of the Kurds was led by Prince Badr Khan in 1847. There is not sufficient information for a definite assessment of the complexities of this revolt, but a tentative assessment is possible.

The family of Badr Khan of Bohtan laid claim to the entire region of Jazira Ibn Omar. In 1843, a vassal of the prince, Nurullah Bey, pillaged the Nestorian Christians of Hakkâri, which led them to protest to Constantinople. In response, Prince Badr Khan joined Nurullah Bey in laying waste to the Nestorian canton of Barwari. The European powers then came to the aid of their coreligionists and compelled the Turks to defend their Christian subjects, which they did by sending an army, under Osman Pasha, against the prince and Nurullah Bey in 1847. Osman defeated the two, and Badr Khan was deported to Crete.[20]

The rising of Nurullah and Badr Khan is of particular significance because it marks a transition from the old-style practice of pure landgrabbing (such as Kor Mohammad engaged in) to something more sinister: confessional massacres perpetrated by religious fanatics. Protestant missionaries had infiltrated the region, and some of them were heavy handedly inciting the Christian tribes against the Turkish authorities in Constantinople.

Badr Khan's attacks on the members of the Nestorian, or Assyrian, church were probably ad hoc affairs but it was not always to be thus because within a few years such confessional massacres became a feature of official Turkish policy. In effect, the authorities in Constantinople deliberately incited the Kurds in order to produce specific political results. Edward Robinson, in the introduction to Sir Austen Henry Layard's *Nineveh* (1849), charges that the Turks incited the Kurds against the Christians with the intention of then destroying the Kurds.

Once Badr Khan was deported to Crete (where he died), the Turks moved resolutely to incorporate Iraq into the central administration of the empire. This was the second phase of their detribalization effort, and it represented a sharp shift in tactics.

The Introduction of Private Property Ownership. The new arrangement mandated settling the Kurds on the land, where they would be more readily available for military conscription and for the exaction of taxes. In effect, the Turks proposed selling the beys and *agha*s land formerly held communally by the tribes.[21] The proposed prices were extremely moderate as the intent was not to realize a cash return but to turn the patriarchal tribal leaders into landlords and the tribesmen into tenants. It would be in each chief's interest to see that the land was worked, but accomplishing this aim would involve a considerable amount of coercion, and given the independence and utterly intractable nature of the tribesmen, the chief-turned-landlord could not hope to exploit his tenants without support of the central government. In the long run, then, the chiefs would be driven into the arms of the central authorities, and also they would be literally driven off the land—that is, they would become absentee landlords—for it would no longer be safe for them to reside close to their erstwhile clansmen. In general, this is how detribalization could be brought about once private property relations had been introduced.

The new category of land tenure was called *tapu*.[22] State land was conditionally allotted to individuals, but it reverted to the state if not used for at least three years. The land was heritable and could be sold to other individuals; therefore it was practically private property.

The Kurds of this period, however, were not accustomed to the idea of private property. Possessing anything meant running the risk of having it appropriated by a more powerful person or group, and prior to the 1830s, there had been no incentive to acquire private property because security of tenure was not assured. In 1829, however, the British threw official support behind a scheme of the East India Company to survey the Euphrates River for possible commercial exploitation by steamboat.[23] The British government's interest was strategic because in accordance with the 1828 Treaty of Turkumanchai the Russians had extracted large concessions from the Persians, and the Russian presence in the Gulf region was becoming intrusive. Were the Euphrates to prove practicable for steam travel, the British could dispatch troops to India more speedily than by sending them via the long sea route around the Cape of Good Hope.

Ultimately, the Euphrates did not prove suitable for travel, but the Tigris River route was opened up to steam travel by the Lynch Company in 1840, which had the effect of introducing a market economy into Iraq, a country previously given over to subsistence agriculture. With improved communications, Iraq could now develop the cash crops of dates and rice in the south and tobacco in the north. Thus, around 1858, when the Turks proposed reassigning Iraqi land on a basis of near-private property rights, the land had begun to have commercial value.

The Kurdish *agha*s did not necessarily immediately appreciate the fact that the land's value had increased and therefore rush to avail themselves of the Turkish government's proposal. Indeed, Longrigg points out that the public's response to the offer was "faint."

Many saw the clear purpose of detribalizing; more suspected any blessing that issued from the [state]; and more were still too well content with their own remoteness to accept a change. Vivid fear of conscription kept the tribes from accepting the obligations of settlement. There was in any case money to be paid. The majority of tribal leaders feared and shunned the new status.[24]

But as Longrigg goes on to say, "the seed was sown." The avarice of the *agha*s (and of the Arab shaikhs to the south since the offer was not restricted to Kurdistan) would ultimately prove telling.

The Era of Anarchy and Expansion

Because of the rather erratic way in which the land reform was carried out, its effect was disguised. There was the outward appearance of order, but underneath, great violence lurked, and the situation could hardly have been otherwise. The rule of the old princes of Kurdistan had been crude and arbitrary, but over the centuries, the arrangement had become systematized; tribesmen and *miskīn* alike knew where they stood. With the coming of external administration, relationships within Kurdish society were turned upside down. The Turks policed the region with a gendarmerie, the Dhabtiyya, but it was hopelessly corrupt.[25] Its officers were usually illiterate; its rank and file, underpaid and ill equipped. Supposedly, justice under the Turkish government was more impersonal than under the old pashas, but with the right of appeal, justice in fact served the rich: They could appeal until satisfied while the poor were pushed aside.

In such situations, when the old way suddenly counts for nothing and the new is but imperfectly understood, power alignments shift, and individuals and institutions that can play one world off against the other thrive. In the commercial sphere entrepreneurs appear, and in politics a new type of leader is called forth. With the breakdown of the established order, the way is prepared for a charismatic leader.

Charismatic Leadership

Because of existing anarchy and confusion, the charismatic leader acts as a magnet, drawing to him people who find the prevailing disorder unbearable. In Kurdistan at the end of the nineteenth century, there were two general types of charismatic leader: the religious leader and the robber baron.

The first, the religious category, was made up of Sufi shaikhs. Because these men affected the course of Kurdish history to the extent that they did, it is necessary to examine briefly the phenomenon of Sufism.

In Kurdistan, Sufism exerts—or did exert—a powerful hold, so much so that it is possible to break down the whole of Iraq into three major religious tendencies: the established Sunnism in the middle region, the militant Shiism in the south, and Sufism in Kurdistan.[26] The first two are recognized sects of Islam; Sufism is an approach to practicing the religion. Originally, Sufism was a form of quietism, but as we shall see, it was anything but that when practiced by the Kurds.

During the reign of Abdul Hamid II (from 1876 to 1909), the Sufis were entrenched at the sultan's court, and in fact, a rather sharp division had grown up. The traditional ulama (religious scholars), having taken on themselves the mission of safeguarding the purity of Islam, distanced themselves from the corrupt courts of the later sultans, which left the field of intrigue to the Sufis. Among the foremost Sufi shaikhs were men of Kurdistan.

Shaikhs Said and Mahmud of Barzinja in Iraq, Shaikh Obaidullah of Shamdinan (northern Iraq), and later Shaikh Said of Turkey and Shaikh Ahmad of Barzan (also in northern Iraq)—almost all had connections at the court of Abdul Hamid, and the fall of that unhappy ruler, which was engineered by the secularist Young Turks, undercut the power of these Kurdish shaikhs. This factor should be kept in mind when trying to account for the delayed appearance of a Kurdish nationalist movement. Nationalism is a secular creed. The Kurds, with their heavy involvement with Sufism and their original strong support of the sultan/caliph, were traditional to the core.

In Kurdistan the Sufi orders with the largest followings are the Qadiri and the Naqshbandi. The former was founded by a famous saint, Shaikh Abdul Qadir al-Gilani (1077–1166).[27] The Path (way of indoctrination) was highly respectable, and in Iraq, until 1960, a descendant of the founder always held the office of primate and keeper of the tomb in Baghdad. Under the Turks the primate was styled Naqib al-Ashraf, and this office was continued under the British. The Kurdish members of the Naqshbandi order, founded by Muhammad Baha-ud-Din of Bukhara (1317–1389), are particularly prone to eccentricity.[28] Both the Qadiri and the Naqshbandi orders are part of the Sunni branch of Islam.

The Barzinja shaikhs, of whom Shaikh Mahmud (b. 1880), the so-called king of Kurdistan, is the most famous in recent times, were of the Qadiri order.[29] At the time of Rich's visit to as-Sulaymaniyah in 1820, Shaikh Maruf Al Nudhi, great-great-grandfather of Shaikh Mahmud, was just achieving prominence. Shaikh Maruf's son Kak Ahmad succeeded him and gained a considerable reputation as a miracle worker, but it is with Mahmud's father, Said, that we are concerned in this chapter, for it was he who filled the vacuum created by the decline of the Babans.

Shaikh Said. The fullest source available for assessing Shaikh Said's career is Major E. B. Soane.[30] He and Shaikh Mahmud were adversaries, and there is good evidence that the shaikh would have murdered Soane—had he not missed his chance—during one stormy episode in their association.[31] However, Soane's evaluation of Shaikh Said was published in 1912 prior to his encounter with Shaikh Mahmud. Soane's experience with the Barzinja shaikhs began when he made a journey in disguise through Kurdistan, during which time he paid a visit to as-Sulaymaniyah.

Soane lays the blame for the serious decline in that city's material position squarely on the Barzinjas, particularly Shaikh Said.[32] The rape, as he styles it, came about in this manner: The strong rule of the old Baban pashas had kept the shaikhs more or less in restraint, but when that rule ended, the shaikhs, by a "successful combination of violence and diplomacy," asserted their power in the area around as-Sulaymaniyah. Shaikh Said was summoned to Constantinople, where he found favor with Abdul Hamid, and from that time on, his fortune and that of his large family were made.

In 1881, the shaikh's tyranny led to a revolt by the as-Sulaymaniyahns. They beseeched the Kurdish Hamawand tribe to assist them in throwing the shaikhs out, and the tribe obliged by surrounding the city. Shaikh Said and his people held out, however, until the siege was lifted by government forces, and those forces then joined the shaikh in exacting his revenge on the city's leading merchants. The shaikh also threw open his doors so that anyone who wished might claim his protection. "In this way," says Soane, "all the worthless members of the population became adherents of the priests."[33]

As the shaikh's control tightened, the city's commerce died. Large sums of money were extorted from the wealthy on any pretext, and shops began to shut. The shaikh purchased nearly all the gardens about the town and then levied a 300 percent duty on fruit coming into the city. That, says Soane, induced every cultivator around to set fire to his orchards and destroy his irrigation works.[34]

In 1908, young Turkish officers (the Young Turks) seized power in Constantinople and compelled Abdul Hamid to restore the Constitution. Shaikh Said rebelled against the Young Turks. According to Soane, Shaikh Said's death soon after was a result of Young Turk duplicity as they lured him to Mosul where he was detained and then murdered. At the time of his death, he owned a considerable amount of land, including the entire marketplace of as-Sulaymaniyah. Shaikh Said's son Mahmud tightened the family's hold over the city, and the Barzinjas remained powerful until 1958. When the revolution began in that year, the family owned one-quarter of the marketplace, and the other three-quarters were municipally owned;[35] Batatu lists 71,716 *dunums* of land in the family's name, all in the province of as-Sulaymaniyah.[36]

Ibrahim Pasha. The second type of leader, the robber baron, approximates the feudal lord of Europe. One such was Ibrahim Pasha of the Milli Kurds of Syria and southern Anatolia. He was a tribal leader, but one whose family had become impoverished as a result of imprudent alliances (Ibrahim's grandfather supported the Egyptian Ibrahim Pasha against the Turks). Father and son rebuilt the fortunes of their tribe, eventually assembling it in the area around Viranshehr north of Diyarbakir.

Ibrahim Pasha's rise occurred mainly during the period when Abdul Hamid II was attempting to reassert the power of the sultan. Ibrahim seems to have profited by the sultan's need for sturdy allies drawn from the ranks of new men who would be entirely beholden to him. After Ibrahim had begun to build a confederacy of Circassians and Arab shaikhs from lesser tribes, Abdul Hamid enrolled him into his Hamadiya cavalry corps and conferred on him the rank of brigadier general and pasha. During the great Armenian massacres of 1895–1896, Ibrahim protected the Armenians in his area[37] and incorporated them into his growing confederacy. He fought the two most powerful Arab tribes, the Anaiza and Shammar, and was able to hold out against both by manipulating their clan rivalries.

Ibrahim's stronghold at Viranshehr began to attract caravan traffic, which Ibrahim encouraged, and his standing at the court in Constantinople reached its highest point. Throughout the period of the rise of the Young Turks, Ibrahim remained Abdul Hamid's man, and, when the constitution was proclaimed, rose in revolt.[38] Ibrahim was killed shortly after, and his confederation was dispersed.

Both Ibrahim Pasha and Shaikh Said began their career-building operations during a period of extraordinary effervescence in the history of Turkey. Mahmud II and the sultans who succeeded him had instituted various reforms, which, imposed mainly by force, had not really taken hold before the reign of Abdul Hamid when the Turkish empire was rocked by its defeat by the Russians.[39] The takeover by the Young Turks was an attempt to force the reform program through at all costs; thus Abdul Hamid, in opposing the Young Turks, was championing reaction.

Lutsky says that the Kurds were the backbone of Abdul Hamid's regime,[40] which means they were also the mainstay of reaction. This statement sums up their role during the period of anarchy between the reform campaigns of Mahmud II and the defeat of Abdul Hamid. Mahmud II swept the old society of the Kurdish princes away, and in the ensuing anarchy a new group of determined opportunists appeared. These men—the Shaikh Saids and the Ibrahim Pashas—joined with Abdul Hamid in trying to preserve the old ways.

The Wolves of Kurdistan

The period of anarchy in Kurdistan fostered the emergence not only of the charismatic leader but also of the lawless tribe, one that kept its cohesion and merely enlarged the scope of its activities when the old petty principalities broke up. One such tribe was notorious throughout the period leading up to World War I and immediately after: the Hamawand, the so-called Wolves of Kurdistan.

Just as the shaikhs had been held in check by the former princes, so too had the wilder tribes. Freed of that restraint, tribes like the Hamawand became a scourge and were absolutely irrepressible. From the standpoint of preserving Kurdish identity in the Middle East, such tribes were probably as important as the charismatic leaders of that crucial interregnum. Sir Mark Sykes, in his registry of Kurdish tribes compiled in 1905, gives the following description of the Hamawand:

> *Hamawand.* 1,200 families. The most valiant, courageous and intelligent of the Baban Kurd tribes. Splendid horsemen, crack shots, capable smiths, bold robbers, good agriculturists, such as enter the government service prove capable officials.

In 1878, 600 Hamawand horsemen armed only with lances penetrated far into the Caucuses [*sic*], and brought back immense spoils. The Turkish government has of late years done much to suppress this tribe's power, but the men are still famous for their prowess and intelligence, and the women for their beauty.[41]

This description is the sort of exaggeration about the Kurds that one encounters frequently in Western literature. It makes the whole people creatures of romance and, in the process, obscures the essential fact about the Hamawand and similar tribes: The Hamawand was not a collection of individuals. It was from the group's "tribliness" that the power of the unit derived, so it formed a contrast to the power bases of Shaikh Said and Ibrahim Pasha, which were preeminently collections of individuals.

Shaikh Said and Ibrahim Pasha each operated during a time of lawlessness when society was disrupted and individuals set adrift. The shaikh's "retainers" were, in Soane's words, "those worthless members of the population,"[42] and Ibrahim Pasha also established his power base on "less respectable elements." When Sykes visited the pasha at his desert camp, he found a crowd of people of every creed and race in the Ottoman Empire. "The Pasha finds [the desert law of hospitality] convenient. For those whose lives are forfeit must stand or fall by their protector and form a dependable bodyguard."[43] In other words, Ibrahim's retinue was composed of desperate individuals. The Hamawand was something completely different. It was a homogeneous unit rather than a collection of self-interested desperadoes, and its members did not follow any charismatic leader—the significant actor was the whole tribe.

The Hamawand inhabited the Bazyan Valley north of as-Sulaymaniyah. Soane says that, strictly speaking, their grounds were outside Kurdistan's western marches.[44] There, in close association with the plains dwellers, the Hamawand intermarried with the Arabs. Perhaps as a result, they were supposed to not resemble Kurds. Although they claimed Arab origin, the Hamawand came originally from Persia, from Qasr-e-Shirin near the frontier. The tribe was always a great trouble to the Persians in spite of being subsidized in an attempt to keep it in control. When Turks ultimately claimed the Hamawand, the Persians handed the tribe over gladly. The Hamawand was never a large tribe. In 1834, it numbered fewer than 500 or 600 families, and yet it was said to be the terror of the Jaf, a tribe of 10,000 to 12,000 tents.

In 1837, the Hamawand was in open rebellion against the Turks, and in 1844 it was plundering between Khanaqin and Qasr-e-Shirin. In 1892, a British traveler said he had some difficulty procuring guides for the trip to as-Sulaymaniyah as the road was closed by raiding parties of Hamawand Kurds and "the whole country was in terror of them, so that almost everywhere the villagers took [the] party for Hamawands and turned out to resist."[45] Edmonds has collected other references to the ferocious tribesmen, the most famous being the story of their deportation to Tripoli. In 1880, the Turks are supposed to have trapped a section of the tribe by treachery and transported them; however, they fought their way back from Africa in six months.[46]

The phenomena of charismatic leaders and the lawless tribe obviously have features in common, but there is a significant difference as well: Only one of them survived the fall of Abdul Hamid. Shaikh Said, by taking advantage of changes in the land code of 1858, which enabled him to buy up large tracts of land, solidified the position of his family, the Barzinjas. Shaikh Said represents the new type of man who was to dominate Kurdish life in the twentieth century: He was the tribal chief–*cum*–landlord, the pivotal figure without whom full private property relations could not have been introduced, as they eventually were under the British.

The Hamadiya

At the end of the nineteenth century, the Kurds became associated with another famous—or, rather, notorious—institution, the Hamadiya cavalry, and because of this association, much opprobrium is attached to the Kurdish name. The cavalry, described as a "yeomanry frontier guard," was the sultan's own unit, serving at his pleasure, and was made up of Kurds and Turkomans.[47] As history has come to emphasize, the Hamadiya's main occupation was massacring Armenians. These massacres were not in the tradition of the earlier confessional disturbances; they were something new insofar as they were deliberate acts of government policy. They were not spontaneous bloodlettings but well-calculated responses by Abdul Hamid to the Russians' nationalist agitation of the Armenians.

The Russians had been manipulating the idea of nationalism throughout the Balkans and had met with great success in Bulgaria, where Slavic committees had exploited racial and religious antagonisms to serve their particular cause.[48] Now, in northeastern Anatolia, revolutionary Armenian committees aggravated divisions between the Muslims and their own Armenian people, as the Bulgarians had done. It was to check this agitation that Abdul Hamid formed the Hamadiya. In effect, he organized the reaction to the Armenian "revolution."

The Kurds who cooperated with Abdul Hamid's reaction were by no means typical of the people as a whole. For centuries, Muslim Kurds and Armenian Christians had lived peaceably together in the northeastern part of Kurdistan, and many of these ties held firm during the period of the massacres as Kurds protected Armenians from the terror. Even when Kurds were the instruments of applying the "grand terror," they were not always allowed to do so without opposition from within their own community. As individual Kurds and whole tribes enlisted in the sultan's cavalry, they antagonized the Kurds who held back,[49] and tribe was set against tribe.

There is no question that the Kurds played a conspicuous part in the massacres following that of Sasun, a mountainous area in Turkey, in 1894, but the point to keep in mind is that the massacres were a part of those grand changes that were affecting the whole area. Since 1829, the Russians had been encroaching on the region, encouraging elements of the Armenian community in the belief that they could have an independent state under the protection of Russia. This encroachment made the Muslim Kurds who inhabited the same area uneasy, so when the Armenians attracted the sympathies of the European powers after the Russo-Turkish war of 1877–1878, the two peoples became bitterly hostile. Had the local Kurds clashed independently with the Armenians, the disturbances of the 1890s would have been part of the pattern of the past: isolated incidents ignited by the fanaticism of the priests. But the Armenian massacres were government sponsored and directed by Ottoman officials. These massacres may be said to have been part of the coming age of nationalism, in which racial and religious differences were exploited to achieve specific political outcomes.

Estimates of how many Armenians lost their lives in the troubles vary between 6,000 and 200,000.[50] Because the Armenian revolutionaries failed (largely for want of great-power support, which they had assumed would be forthcoming), whole areas of the northeast were cleared of Armenians, and the Kurds' geographic spread continued into these areas at the turn of the century.

The Kurds at the End of the Nineteenth Century

The last of the great Kurdish revolts of the nineteenth century was that led by Shaikh Obaidullah. Kurdish nationalists claim this revolt was a nationalist rising, but, in fact, it was clearly tied into the policies of Abdul Hamid and also the rivalry of the great powers in the region. As such, it foreshadowed Kurdish involvement with other movements of nationalism—Arab, Turk, Persian—which were to dominate the twentieth century.

Shaikh Obaidullah of Shamdinan revolted in 1880, not against the Turks but against the Persians. Some commentators suggest that the shaikh's threat to set up an independent Kurdish, Muslim principality in part of Persia actually was directed at the Russians to discourage their intriguing for an independent Armenian, Christian state in Turkish territory.[51] According to this interpretation, the shaikh was not his own man but a pawn of the sultan.

The specific grievance that incited Shaikh Obaidullah was a raid by Persian troops into Turkish Kurdistan. Some young Kurds were killed, others kidnapped. The shaikh, in retaliation, ravaged the districts of Urmia, Sawdj-Bujak, Mir-Jando-Ab, and Maragha in today's Iran. He then marched on Tabriz. Kurdish nationalists offer as proof of the shaikh's nationalist sentiments a letter he is supposed to have written arguing that

> the Kurdish nation is a people apart. . . . Whether Turkish or Persian subjects . . . one and all are united and agreed that matters cannot be carried on this way with the two governments, and that necessarily something must be done so that the European governments having understood the matter shall enquire into our state.[52]

The rhetoric is impressive; it is the subsequent career of the shaikh that is troubling. Just when his movement was on the point of success, he abandoned it. Some writers suggest that Anglo-Russian pressure on the Turks forced them to coerce Obaidullah into giving up the revolt, but others say that the Turks, once they persuaded the Russians to forgo their Armenian venture, simply canceled the operation. Shaikh Obaidullah was called by the sultan to Constantinople where he was briefly imprisoned until he escaped to his home district. Recaptured, he was transported to Mecca where he died.

With the elimination of Shaikh Obaidullah, it appeared on the surface that the Kurds had fared badly in the nineteenth century: All of their principalities—the glorious remembrance of today's Kurdish nationalists—had been smashed. In fact, however, the Kurds had thrived under Abdul Hamid. The shaikhs and ruthless individuals like Ibrahim Pasha formed nothing less than the backbone of the sultan's regime, and they were rewarded. By early 1900, the Kurds had spread as far west as Ankara and had also encroached into the northeastern corner of the Anatolian peninsula where the Armenians dwelt. It was only in the south, because of the inhospitability of the desert, that their spread was balked. In terms of numbers and the area occupied, the Kurds had done very well. Without their knowing it, however, all their gains were subject to forfeit. An idea was to call all into question—the idea of nationalism.

3
The First Stirrings
of Nationalism

Over the course of centuries, a fine balance of coexistence had developed among the peoples in the region around Kurdistan—the Kurds, Armenians, Assyrians, Turks, Persians, and Arabs—but before World War I, this harmony began to fray. The first peoples to be uprooted by the war were the Assyrians and the Armenians, and their dislocation profoundly affected the Kurds. The period immediately following World War I was one of great nationalist agitation in the Middle East. Inevitably, the fever of nationalism infected the Kurds, but it was not initially a native movement as the idea was introduced by the British. Compared to other groups in the area, the Kurds began nationalist agitation rather late. Nevertheless, the movement gathered strength, and as it did so, it became the Kurds' only hope of preserving themselves from extinction.

The Kurdistan Minorities

It is not well known, in the West at least, how World War I ravaged the eastern Anatolian region. The army of the czar initially penetrated quite far south—the Russian front running south from Trabzon through Lake Van and Kurdistan to Rawanduz[1] and the southern parts of Azerbaijan.[2] Military action against the minorities occurred in a seesaw fashion. First, the Russians marched into the Kurdish region around

Lake Urmia, where they were resisted by some 3,000 Kurds of the Shikak tribe. Russian arms prevailed, and the Shikak, under their chief, the redoubtable Simko, fell back into Turkey. The Russians ultimately pushed beyond lakes Urmia and Van, completely clearing the provinces of Van, Bitlis, and Erzurum. The Armenians in this region (reduced in number by the earlier Hamadiya massacres) joined up with the Russians, and the local Kurds retreated south to Mosul and west to Diyarbakir and Konia. The Russians did not hold the area for long, but during their occupation, they despoiled the Muslim territories—living off the land, destroying irrigation works, and burning orchards.[3] In the winter of 1917, the Bolsheviks overthrew the czarist government, the Russian front collapsed, and the Turks and the Kurds returned. The Armenians fled north after the retreating czarist troops, whose departure (after the armistice between the Bolsheviks and the Turks was confirmed in December 1917) unleashed further devastation—famine followed by epidemic. But all these troubles were nothing compared to those caused by the confessional strife that ensued.

The Assyrians

The Assyrians, although Christians, were not closely tied to the Russians (their links were with the Protestant British), but they were still more or less stranded by the czarist troops' retreat. There were two major communities of Assyrians, one in Iran and one in Turkey. The Iranian Assyrians (who technically were neutral because Iran stayed out of World War I) lived in the plain around Rezaiyeh; the Turkish Assyrians, the Jelu, lived in the mountains. The warlike Jelu, numbering 25,000, had been armed by the Russians, and they fled their homes when their protectors retreated[4] and joined the 25,000 Iranian Assyrians around Rezaiyeh. The unexpected appearance of the Jelu upset the balance of Muslims and Christians in the region, and a major tragedy was in the making.

The collapse of the Russian front severely compromised the allies. Just prior to the czarist regime's dissolution, German forces had struck deeply into the Caucasus, landing troops at Batum with the intent of seizing the oil fields at Baku. In 1917, the British, determined to repulse the German move on Baku, sent an expeditionary force under Major General L. C. Dunsterville into the southern Caucasus region.

There is no point in retelling the story of the "Dunsterforce"; it is of interest here only insofar as it directly exacerbated the "minorities question." General Dunsterville had hoped to find reinforcements for his tiny force (numbering only fourteen officers and forty-one trucks) from among the cadres of the retreating Russians,[5] but they refused to be enticed into joining him. The general next looked to the Assyrian refugees, and here he met with better success. The Assyrians claimed the respect of the British for several quite compelling reasons, the main one being that these Jelu were mountaineers and were therefore accustomed to the terrain of the high Zagros. Further, they were used to fighting Kurds, who, along with the Turks, might be expected to oppose the Dunsterforce. It must have seemed serendipitous to Dunsterville that these hardy mountaineers should have been so conveniently available. The Assyrians joined the Dunsterforce, but it was a marriage of desperation. Dunsterville had miscalculated the Russians' willingness to be associated with the Baku scheme, which could not go forward without some reinforcement. The Assyrians could not go back as the Kurds were there thirsting for vengeance—they had to go forward.

Eventually, disaster befell the whole Dunsterforce campaign, including the Assyrians. General Dunsterville had arranged to have the Assyrians supplied with weapons and ammunition to facilitate wide-ranging operations against the Turks, but this supply operation failed.[6] One element of the Assyrian force, under Agha Petros, missed the supply drop scheduled by the British air corps and impulsively turned south, deserting the main body under its spiritual-temporal leader, the Mar

Shimoun.* The Agha Petros unit successfully fought its way to British lines, but the main group was not so lucky. The Mar Shimoun decided that he and his followers would stay where they were around Rezaiyeh. To conciliate the Kurdish Shikak, the principal tribe of that region, he invited its leader, Simko, to a parley. Simko accepted, only to fall upon the Assyrians and massacre them. The remnants of the force retreated south to British protection, but they were harassed all the way by attacking Kurds. William Eagleton writes: "Though it was not fully realized at the time, the Assyrian nation had been destroyed"[7]—even though total annihilation did not occur until 1931.

The Armenians

A little later, after World War I, the Armenians fared almost as badly as the Assyrians. The style of their passing differed, however, for they were able briefly to set up their own republic. The Kurds were not a direct party to the Armenian destruction, which was accomplished by the Turks and the Bolsheviks, and, indeed, at the Paris Peace Conference a Kurdish leader, one of the Babans, and the Armenian delegation worked to coordinate the claims of the two peoples against the Turks.[8] Initially, the Armenians seemed to be, along with the Zionists, the chief beneficiaries among the minorities of the Allies' peace proposals as an area was set aside in northeastern Anatolia and the Transcaucasus for the establishment of an Armenian republic. However, just as the inordinate delay in signing the peace treaty between the Allies and Turkey wrecked British plans for the Iraqi Kurds, it also adversely affected the Armenians. Mustafa Kemal (Ataturk) used the long interval to work out a concerted action with the Bolsheviks to crush the vulnerable Armenian republic, and the end came in September 1920 when the Kemalists struck from the south and the Bolsheviks from the northeast. The Armenians held

---

*Mar Shimoun is a hereditary title held by successive Assyrian leaders.

out briefly, but by December, the republic was finished. Thus, another nation in that part of the world passed into oblivion.

Shaikh Obaidullah of Shamdinan is supposed to have said, "The Turks need us [the Kurds] only as a counterbalance to the Christians and when there are no Christians, they will turn the reprisals on ourselves."[9] He is said to have made this statement after being importuned by the Turks to undertake another massacre of Christians, and his refusal expressed a deep understanding of the function of ethnic diversity in the Ottoman Empire. The minorities served to police each other; had they combined, they might have smashed the Turks. But of course the Turks saw to it that they did not unite by always aggravating their mutual grievances and then stepping in to preserve the losers before the victors could eliminate them.

British-Sponsored Kurdish Nationalism

At the end of World War I, the British introduced the idea of Kurdish nationalism, and the Treaty of Sèvres (August 1920), whereby Britain and Turkey first tried to conclude their hostilities after the war, contained two articles relating to the Kurds. Article 62 provided for local autonomy in a part of eastern Anatolia where the Kurds constituted a majority. Article 64 read as follows:

> If within one year from the coming into force of the present Treaty the Kurdish peoples within the areas defined in Article 62 shall address themselves to the Council of the League of Nations in such a manner as to show that a majority of the population of these areas desires independence from Turkey, and if the Council then considers that it should be granted to them, Turkey hereby agrees to execute such a recommendation, and to renounce all rights and title over these areas. . . . If and when such renunciation takes place, no objection will be raised by the principal Allied Powers to the voluntary adhesion to such an independent Kurdish State of the Kurds inhabiting that part of Kurdistan which has hitherto been included in the Mosul *wilayat* ["province"].

These two articles form the basis of the Kurdish nationalists' claims to an independent state of Kurdistan as they explicitly recognize that the Kurds exist as a people and that they are entitled to a separate state. However, the treaty was never ratified because the successes of Mustafa Kemal, in particular his defeat of the Greeks in the summer of 1921, led the Turks to repudiate it. The British made no attempt to write the articles into the Treaty of Lausanne, which Turkey and Britain signed in 1923, because the British had changed their position on the Kurds. They now wanted to annex Mosul (actually southern Kurdistan) to their newly created client state of Iraq.

There are various theories as to why the British changed their minds. One has to do with oil. It was obvious from their renegotiation in 1918 of the 1916 Sykes-Picot Agreement that the British had known for some time that there was oil in Kirkuk, part of the Mosul *wilayet*. According to the original agreement, France would have acquired possession of Mosul, but after an agreement between Clemenceau and Lloyd George in 1918, Britain obtained control of Mosul, and France received a share of the region's oil production. The theory is that Mosul was all the British were really interested in. They could secure the oil just as well by incorporating the area into their client state of Iraq; they had no need to create a ministate of Kurdistan.

A second theory is that British occupation of Iraq—plus Mosul—was the brainchild of the India Office, which had been responsible for British military operations in the Gulf area throughout World War I. The India Office wished to establish a protectorate over what was then called Mesopotamia, but it was mindful that the protectorate, Iraq, would not be viable unless Mosul were added to the two Mesopotamian *wilayet*s of Baghdad and Basrah.[10]

A third theory has to do with the schemes of Britain's foreign secretary, Lord Curzon. Curzon supported an aggressive policy in Iran after the collapse of the Russian front brought about by the Bolsheviks' overthrow of the czar. "The manifest aim," writes Temperley, "was to draw a cordon across Persia to prevent German, Turkish or Bolshevik agencies from reaching Afghanistan on the Indian frontier and sewing [*sic*] dissension there."[11] Temperley goes on to say that under the policy worked out by the home government "Mesopotamia was intended to be held in conjunction with Persia. . . . as a military measure the capture of Baghdad or even of Mosul may have been sound, but the establishment of civil administration confronted us with problems of quite another order."[12] Temperley makes the point that Curzon's policy meant keeping communication lines open through Mosul and stationing 100,000 British and colonial troops in Iraq, whereas before the war the Turks had controlled the region with a maximum of 12,000 men.[13] The British had to surmount substantial obstacles in order to acquire and hold Mosul.

Britain first landed troops in present-day Iraq at Fao at the mouth of the Shatt al-Arab on November 6, 1914, and they remained in Iraq for the four years of the war with Turkey. On October 30, 1918, the armistice was signed at Mudros between the Turks and the British, who had pushed their line forward to the high road between Khanaqin (in Iraq near the border with Iran west of Kermanshah) and Altun-Kupri (between Kirkuk and Irbil). Of the towns between, Kirkuk, which had been captured on May 7, 1918, and then abandoned, was retaken only five days before the armistice. Mosul fell on November 3, four days after the armistice, which drew sharp protests from Turkey.[14] From November 3 on, the question of Mosul, and indeed of all Kurdistan, was tied up until September 30, 1924, when the League of Nations appointed a three-man commission composed of a Swede, a Hungarian, and a Belgian to oversee the holding of a referendum by the people of Mosul.

Several commentators felt the referendum scheme ill advised. Referenda may be a suitable means of measuring public opinion in a democracy, but in the mountains of Kurdistan they clearly are not so effective. Nevertheless, Edmonds, among other British political officers in the region, labored hard to deliver the Kurdish vote in favor of incorporation into the state of Iraq.

The British faced some formidable obstacles. First, there was the unfortunate recollection of Kirkuk. By capturing the town on May 7, 1918, and leaving it seventeen days later, the British had severely compromised all the people there who had welcomed them after the Turks retreated. Among the people who had been left at the mercy of the reoccupying Turks were the Hamawand tribesmen. They and other Kurds could not be persuaded afterward that the British and their clients, the Sharifian government of Baghdad, were back there to stay.[15] The bulk of the population, drawing on centuries of experience of their Turkish overlords, favored a return to Turkish control because Kurdistan had always been ruled by Turks—who always dealt harshly with renegades.

In September 1925, the three-man League of Nations commission delivered its report, which favored including all of the Mosul *wilayet* up to the present border with Turkey in the Iraqi state. Influential in the commissioners' decision was the solid support for Iraq encountered in as-Sulaymaniyah, that is, southern Kurdistan. The Kurds there seemed to have been won over by an economic argument: The bulk of the city's trade was oriented south and west toward Baghdad and Aleppo. Nevertheless, the as-Sulaymaniyahns still had reservations about coming under exclusively Arab control. The commission specified that the British mandate for Iraq must be held for at least twenty years, Kurdish officials must be appointed for the Kurdish areas, and Kurdish must be the official language; otherwise, the disputed territory should be partitioned along the Little Zab River. After some hesitation, the Turks accepted the commission's recommendations on June 5, 1926, when a treaty was signed in Ankara between Britain, Turkey, and Iraq. Mosul became part of Iraq, and Britain and Turkey ended their "unnatural estrangement" after eleven years.

Gertrude Bell is one commentator who believes the British never should have agreed to a referendum,[16] because by doing so, they guaranteed the growth of nationalism in the region. She quotes the Naqib (a family descended from the Prophet) of Baghdad: "We should have been spared the folly of asking people to express their wish as to the future. It was been the cause of great unrest."[17] Indeed, conventional wisdom holds that prior to the close of World War I, nationalism was the furthest thing from the Kurds' minds. Sir Arnold Toynbee gives a Turkish view: The Kurds are "a people in a clan stage of development who have scarcely begun to acquire a consciousness of national solidarity,"[18] and Sir Arnold Wilson cites an Arab nationalist's contemptuous rejection of the Kurds as "peasants who can be kept in line by the mutual animosities of their chiefs."[19]

The Native Kurdish Nationalist Movement

Thus the British had sown the seed of the Kurdish nationalism, and its subsequent native development was encouraged by several factors, one of which was the Allies' treatment of the Armenians after World War I. The news that the victors intended to found an Armenian republic impressed at least the Kurds of as-Sulaymaniyah, the southern Kurdish "capital," where such intellectuals as existed in Kurdistan were concentrated. These city Kurds were emboldened to think seriously about a free Kurdistan after the Armenian example.

Another factor that must have had a great influence was the appearance of a virulent Arab nationalist movement. Britain was granted the mandate for Iraq late. The armistice was signed at Mudros on October 30, 1918, but Britain did not accept the mandate until April 25, 1920—the delay was occasioned in part by difficulty over French claims to Syria. Colonel T. E. Lawrence of the Arab Bureau had envisioned the creation of three Arab states, each assigned to one of the Hashemite brothers who were leaders of the Arab revolt promoted by Lawrence and the bureau.[20] Originally, the eldest brother, Faisal, was to rule Syria—despite the fact that the British had, in the secret Sykes-Picot Agreement, promised Syria to France. When France ejected Faisal from Syria, a crown was found for him in Iraq in 1921, but this solution was not accomplished expeditiously, and for a time it appeared that a satisfactory arrangement with Faisal might never be worked out. The India Office did not want to see the creation of an independent Arab state of Iraq, which could destroy its scheme for turning that area into a British protectorate. To force the hand of the India Office, Arab supporters of Faisal—the so-called Sharifian faction—launched an Arab revolt in the middle Euphrates River region. By June 1920, this revolt lapped against the borders of Kurdistan when Arab tribes raided Tall 'Afar and murdered the British assistant political officer, Major Barlow.

Shaikh Mahmud's Rebellions

All of these factors—Britain's support in the Treaty of Sèvres of an autonomous Kurdish entity, Allied plans for an Armenian state, and the Arab nationalist agitation next door—influenced the growth of Kurdish nationalism after the war. Still, the Kurds needed a leader who could translate an abstract idea into a cause, and one did appear in the person of Shaikh Mahmud. This was the man chosen by the British to head an independent Kurdistan under the Treaty of Sèvres, but twice he turned on them as he was determined to be his own man.

Shaikh Mahmud Barzinja came from one of the most numerous and influential *sayyid* families of Kurdistan, that is, those who were descended from the Prophet,[21] and it was this noble lineage that recommended Shaikh Mahmud to the British. In fact, the British had negotiated with several illustrious Kurds to head a Kurdish state. Sayyid Taha, the grandson of Shaikh Obaidullah of Shamdinan, was approached, as was one of the Babans. However, Sayyid Taha set too high a price for cooperating, and the Baban spoke no Kurdish and "was more interested in his family's illustrious past than the realities of present-day Iraq."[22] So, in the end, Shaikh Mahmud was chosen.

Shaikh Mahmud seems to have given the British trouble from the first. The original bargain was struck at the war's end by Major E. W. Noel, and the two men seem to have been on good terms. The shaikh's attitude may have been influenced by the generous British offer: Any tribes between the Sirwas and Great Zab rivers wishing to accept his leadership would be allowed to do so. When it became apparent that Mahmud was not so loved as the British had supposed, they restricted his "realm" to the *liwa* ("district") of as-Sulaymaniyah and certain adjacent districts of the *liwa* of Kirkuk.[23] At the same time, Major Noel was reassigned, and a new political officer was attached to the shaikh. This was none other than Major Soane, who had written so unsympathetically of Mahmud's father, Shaikh Said. This double repulse seems to have spurred the shaikh to action, and in June 1919, the *hukmdar* ("king") of as-Sulaymaniyah revolted. Initially, he had the support of his own Barzinja family and elements of the Hamawand and Jaf tribes and the Aoroman tribes in Persia. This last adherence proved a grave complicating factor for the British as they did not want to disrupt relations with Persia. The shaikh's first revolt was short-lived. Within a month, colonial troops, largely Burmese and Indian, had defeated him, and he was seriously wounded in the process. He was then exiled to India.

Britain accepted the mandate for Iraq on April 25, 1920. A British-promoted referendum had been held throughout the country (excluding Mosul) on Faisal's candidacy for the kingship of Iraq, and the result was 90 percent approval. As-Sulaymaniyah had refused to participate, and most of the no votes had come from Kirkuk. This combination added up to an unambiguous rejection of the Sharifian government by the Kurds. Until the matter could be settled, the British high commissioner, Sir Percy Cox, assumed responsibility for the Kurdish areas. However, Cox had surrendered almost all his physical resources to the Iraqi government, the British general headquarters was averse to employing imperial troops in remote areas in which it had no interest, and permission to use locally recruited levies was difficult to obtain. The feeling was that the Kurds had deliberately elected to stay out of the new kingdom and were therefore entitled to no assistance.[24] Nevertheless, British assistant political officers, generally with a thin detachment of thirty to forty men, remained posted in the chief towns of Iraqi Kurdistan through a period of mounting tension. In 1921, the Turks started sending over their own small detachments as reinforcements for the tribes who were being suborned to the Turks' side, and soon the whole area north of Rawanduz, the remotest mountain region of Kurdistan, threatened to erupt. As Edmonds reported when he took over as political officer at Halabjah in 1921, "the area was distinctly jittery."[25]

Because of this charged atmosphere, the British decided to bring back Shaikh Mahmud in September 1922. Their choices were simple: They could force the Kurds into the Iraqi state (which they had solemnly averred they would not do), or they could find some prominent Kurdish personality to rule, someone who would resist Turkish propaganda. As Sayyid Taha once again took himself out of the running, there was no alternative but to return the shaikh. This time, the British took pains to make plain to him the exact lines of his authority.

Nevertheless, in November 1922, Mahmud proclaimed himself king of Kurdistan, and before long, he was secretly dealing with the Turks. At this point, the British, who had despaired of him altogether, called in the Royal Air Force, RAF, which bombed Shaikh Mahmud out of as-Sulaymaniyah. Without effective ground control, however, the British could not keep him from returning, and by July 1923, he was once more in possession of the city. Lacking either the will or the resources to drive him away again, the British erected a cordon around the area. Mahmud was to be allowed to range unchecked within its limits, but any attempt to break the bounds would be rewarded by a "caning."[26] And so the matter rested until 1923. Turkey and Britain were to sign the Treaty of Lausanne in that year, and it would have been extremely awkward to have Shaikh Mahmud still in revolt just then. In July 1924, the British drove him out of Kurdistan permanently.

Kurdish defenders of Mahmud claim the British used him: Set on controlling the Mosul *wilayet,* the British did not hesitate to create "facts" supportive of their position. It is alleged that by establishing Shaikh Mahmud in the "kingship" of an autonomous region, British propagandists provided the essential referent for a lobbying campaign, giving the Kurds of Mosul (who made up five-eighths of the population) an alternative to reincorporation by the Turks. The Turks have countered that they and the Kurds were brothers, which may have been true under the Ottomans but was scarcely the case with the Young Turks and their program of "Turkification." Britain, it is claimed, was never serious about countenancing an independent Kurdistan. Once the Mosul question was arranged to Britain's liking (June 5, 1926) and the British had signed a concession for oil (February 1925), the question of Kurdish rights was dropped, never to be revived by the British.[27]

Given what is known about British and French schemes to partition the Middle East, the Kurdish nationalists' argument is not far-fetched. It is harder, however, to accept their judgment of Shaikh Mahmud specifically. Certainly, the shaikh thought of himself as more than a tribal leader: He set up a government of eighty members, issued postage stamps, levied taxes, and published a newspaper, the *Sun of Kurdistan.* But his appeal does not seem to have been profound, and he could not bind the tribes to him in adversity. In 1923, when the British relinquished the as-Sulaymaniyah region to him, the tribes rallied round, but the tribes were only continuing the centuries-old Kurdish practice of following a successful war leader and deserting him when his luck turned. Under Mahmud, the Kurdish nationalist movement never confronted its major challenge. To hold out against the Iraqis *and* the British, the shaikh would have had to mobilize the Kurds with an appeal to something other than their deep-dyed acquisitiveness. He never did so. Thus the solidarity to accomplish anything lasting was lacking. What the shaikh did do, aside from manipulating some of the symbols of modern nationalism, was provide a cause for later Kurdish nationalists to exploit.

The End of the Empires

After Mahmud, the nationalist movement gained new strength as the Kurds fought to resist the consolidating policies of the new regimes in Turkey and Iran. What was not immediately appreciated following World War I was that there had been a fundamental system-change in the Middle East. The Turkish empire was finished (it was formally abolished in 1922), and the empire of Iran, with its irredentist claims to vast stretches of southern Russia and western Afghanistan and the island of Bahrain in the Gulf, was also in eclipse. In the place of these two moribund empires came nation states. The organizing principle of nation states differs from that of empires. To maintain control over vast stretches of territory that embrace many disparate peoples, empire builders must keep minorities intact and cultivate their mutual animosities; nation states, on the other hand, stand or fall by the solidarity of the people. Thus the organizing principle of the nation state is homogeneity.

The Kurds could not know as early as the end of World War I that the disappearance of the Assyrians and Armenians was not to prove as advantageous as they originally perceived because the Turks and—to a lesser extent—the Iranians had imbibed a new religion: nationalism. This development was to have a profound effect on Turkish-Kurdish relations. The Kurds and Turks were not related racially, and their tie had been one of faith—both groups were Sunni Muslims. Once that bond was ruptured, the Turks had no claim of allegiance to impose upon the Kurds, and with all the zeal of new converts (to the religion of nationalism), the Turks were heedless in destroying the old order. In 1922, Ataturk forced the abdication of the sultan, a move that caused genuine dismay. Hasan Arfa, who traveled through the Kurdish regions of Anatolia in 1922, tells of being questioned by a delegation of Kurdish *agha*s.

"We have heard that the victorious Turkish army has entered Istanbul. What has happened to our Sultan?"

"He abdicated," I said, "and left Istanbul on a British warship."

A deep silence followed, the villagers pondering over what I had said. "Who will be the Sultan then?"

"There will be no Sultan, only a Caliph, and he is the Sultan's cousin. . . ."

"But how is it possible for a country to be without a Sultan?"

"There will be a Republic."

"What is that?" I tried to explain it to them, but they did not or did not want to understand, and kept on saying: "But without a Sultan there could not be a State!"[28]

The confusion of the Kurds over this issue is easily explained. Their only true connection to the Turks was through the institution of the sultan/caliph. He was the "commander of the faithful," and as such was entitled to the fealty of all Muslims. Without him there was no basis for attachment. A state without a sultan was inconceivable to the Kurds. Still, a kind of grudging, conditional allegiance could be accorded to Ankara as long as the caliphate was preserved, but when Ataturk struck that down as well in March 1924, the loyalties of good Muslims were tested to the limit. One year later, Shaikh Said of Dalu in Turkey, hereditary chief of the Naqshbandi sect, rose in rebellion, specifically against the "godless" Ankara government. Most commentators believe the revolt was religiously inspired, but there is evidence the British may have instigated it.[29]

Shaikh Said's Revolt. Just as the British are suspected of having used Shaikh Mahmud for their own purposes, they are also suspected of instigating Shaikh Said's revolt. The timing of the rebellion is what raises these suspicions, as it took place in 1925 just as the League of Nations commission was concluding its deliberations on Mosul. Mosul was predominantly Kurdish, and the commission could not help but be influenced by a major Kurdish upheaval just north of

Mosul in Turkey. As was generally the case with rebellions in this region, the fighting spilled over into the surrounding areas, Mosul included. A stream of Kurdish refugees pouring south to escape Turkish arms did not improve Turkey's case before the commission. The rebellion, once incited, spread with such speed that causes other than religious zeal seemed to be involved. Toynbee suggests that the bad economic situation in the eastern *wilayet*s fed the revolt. He notes that Shaikh Said was wealthy, with large commercial interests, and that Kemal's Turkification policy was aimed in part at stripping the feudalists of their power.[30] According to this interpretation, the revolt was a last-ditch stand of reaction.

Trouble spread in all directions: Siverek, Diyarbakir, Lice, and Mus fell to the rebels, whose numbers swelled beyond the 7,000 who had initially joined the shaikh. At first, the rebels had an unbroken string of successes, which forced the government to proclaim martial law throughout the eastern *wilayet*s. But then the Kurds, for whom warfare was first and foremost a chance to loot, undercut their own gains by terrorizing the villagers in the territory they controlled.[31] With a hostile population surrounding them, the Kurds' operations received a serious check because when the Turkish army pushed north,[32] many villagers joined their ranks. The hostility of the people, who were alienated by the Kurds' excesses, and the sudden appearance of the Turkish troops almost certainly were responsible for the eventual failure of the rebellion.

Modern technology and the railway assisted the Turks. They were armed with superior rifles, their commanders called in air support, and planes strafed columns of Kurds caught on the run. Shaikh Said might ordinarily have hoped to fall back into Iraq or Persia, but he was caught in a ring of some 35,000 Turks. At the beginning of April, the Turkish forces started a general offensive against the insurgents, and after a period of desperate resistance, the Kurds surrendered, and the shaikh was captured. The last remnants of the rebels were rounded up on April 28, 1926. Shaikh Said and nine of his lieutenants were tried, condemned, and hanged; other insurgents were imprisoned for long periods.

The revolt had cost the newly installed government of Ataturk a great deal—it had spent more than £2 million to quell the insurrection,[33]—and Kemel now took steps to avoid a repetition. He ordered the wholesale removal of several tribes from their traditional homes to the Adana region in southwestern Turkey. He specifically transported *aghas* and beys. Where the traditional elite were not disturbed, he undercut their authority by decreeing the abolition of titles. Finally, he ordered compulsory education in the Turkish language. Although detribalization moved slowly at first, it proceeded inexorably. From now on, rebellion in Turkey was marked by desperation as the Kurds struggled to resist the detribalization that was being forced upon them.

Ismail Agha Simko's Revolt. In Iran, Ismail Agha Simko was already in revolt when the transition from empire to nation state took place. The destruction of the Assyrian nation, the collapse of the czarist forces, and the embarrassment of the Allies' Dunsterforce had left Simko, mentioned earlier in connection with the Assyrian massacre, in possession of Iranian territory west of Lake Urmia from Khoi in the north to Saqqez and Baneh in the south. In 1919, this Shikak chieftain led 3,000 armed tribesmen in the area of Azerbaijan, which now was denuded of potential foes, on a course of conquest: His aims were to wrest the area from the control of Tehran and to set up an independent state under his own direction. At this juncture, Iran was still under the suzerainty of the last of the Qajars, an extremely weak regime that would be replaced within a year by that of Reza Khan, Iran's first modernizing autocrat in the style of Ataturk. Simko launched his takeover by seizing Rezaiyeh. His army had collected some field guns left by the retreating czarists and had been joined by some Turkish artillerymen, deserters who had thrown in their lot with him for the salary of one gold Turkish lira a day.[34] Next, in 1920, Simko and some 4,000 men took Shahpur in northwestern Iran, where he experienced a reverse at the hands of Iran's czarist-officered Cossack Brigade. But as the Cossacks did not pursue their victory, Simko remained unsubdued. In fact, that same year he reoccupied all his former territories.

The Iranian government—first under the Qajars and then under Reza Khan (soon to become shah)—sent successive sorties against Simko and harassed him without letup. The rebellion lasted from 1920 until July 1922 when Reza Khan moved two columns against Simko. Arfa's account of this action (which took place just north of Rezaiyeh Lake [Lake Urmia]) is vivid.[35] Arfa, who took part, witnessed the "last charge" of the Kurds, which ended with a Kurdish defeat. Over 10,000 Kurds participated, fighting with swords and daggers and attacking entrenched infantry positions on horseback. However, they were no match for a regular army that was well equipped with modern weapons. After the engagement, Simko fled into Iraq. He was allowed back into Iran in 1925, rebelled again in 1926, and was defeated with the aid of the Turks.

A Theory of Stability

With the end of the empires, a great change had come about in both Turkey and Iran. In Iraq, because of specific policies pursued by the British, the Kurds were more or less left alone. In Turkey and Iran, however, the Kurdish question became a matter of national survival, and henceforth the Kurds would be either assimilated or eliminated wherever possible. It is essential for the reader to appreciate the magnitude of the change. The Armenians, the Assyrians, and the Kurds had existed as nations in the region for centuries. And now, seemingly at a stroke, they either had been swept away or were so threatened as not to have much chance of survival. To explain this sudden turn of affairs I go back to the theory I proposed in the first chapter. When the opposing empires of Russia and Britain concentrated their attention on the area, the border region stabilized. As the great powers relaxed their attention and pressure, the limitrophe region destabilized. In 1918, the Bolsheviks, in effect, drew back. Anxious to dissociate themselves from the war, they conceded to Germany and Turkey vast stretches of territory formerly held by Russia, in particular the region of Kars, Ardehan, and Batum on the present-day Turkish-USSR border. Thus they essentially released these regions from their control. The Germans and the Turks might have taken over had they not lost the war. In the interval between the collapse of the Russian front and the mid-1920s, there were, as we have seen, major destabilizing revolts in Turkey, Iran, and Iraq. By the late 1920s, each of these revolts had been ruthlessly crushed, and stability had returned to the region. This was possible, according to my theory, because of international events: Bolshevik Russia reasserted its influence in the region, and the erstwhile balance between it and Britain was thus reestablished. With the return of the balance came stability, and the instrument for achieving this stability was the nation state, under authoritarian secular control. That change was an unhappy development for the Kurds.

4
The Nation States and the
Reactionary Challenge

During the 1930s, Iran, Turkey, and Iraq continued their development as nation states, and the question of the minorities arose repeatedly. In this chapter, we shall see that during this decade, Reza Shah moved to detribalize the Kurds in Iran, and Ataturk ruthlessly put down a second great rising of the Kurds in Turkey. In Iraq, British policies resulted in general detribalization, and the Assyrians in that country, who mistakenly relied on a British alliance, were massacred by government forces at Simel in northwestern Iraq. We shall also see that a degree of regional cooperation in the region was achieved when Iran, Turkey, and Iraq signed the Saadabad Pact in 1937.

Neither the national nor the regional stability achieved by the nation states during this period favored the Kurdish nationalist movement. Both kinds of stability, however, were definitely in the interests of the two great powers that survived World War I, Britain and the USSR.

Iran

The concern with stability seems such a contrast with the previous requirements of the two powers that a brief review of the diplomacy affecting Iran is in order. George Lenczowski describes the "special understanding" that had motivated Rus-

sian-British dealings in south-central Asia prior to World War
I. For the British,

> the safest way to protect India was to establish on her frontiers
> a chain of territories that would be either under British
> ascendancy or free from the influence of another Big Power.
> Exclusive British ascendancy in the chain of territories con-
> sisting of Iran, Afghanistan, Sin-Kiang, and Tibet was barred
> by Imperial Russia. Accordingly two alternatives remained:
> (a) a shared ascendancy through agreement on Russian and
> British spheres of influence or (b) preservation of the inde-
> pendence of the territories as a political no-man's land between
> Russia and British imperial organisms. Of the two alternatives,
> the British preferred the latter. This preference was based on
> two facts: first, any division of territory would serve as a
> precedent to sanction further Russian penetration toward
> India or the Persian Gulf; hence any British gain would be
> offset by an increased Russian military threat to India;
> secondly, the pacification of the occupied, naturally discon-
> tented regions, would entail effort and expense.... As the
> British viewed it, then, an independent Iran, free from all
> foreign influences was to be preferred to an Iran under shared
> domination of Britain and Russia.[1]

Nevertheless, Britain had agreed to "a shared ascendancy"
with Russia in the 1907 Anglo-Russian Agreement whereby
Iran was divided into spheres of interest. Britain had not been
keen on this arrangement for it gave Russia an advantage,
but there was a war coming on in Europe, and Britain had
viewed Russia as a potential ally. However, once the Russian
front collapsed, Britain returned to the "maximalist" solution:
to set up that chain of territories under British ascendancy
that Lenczowski mentions. The ill-fated Dunsterforce was the
spearhead, and when it failed, Britain still tried to consolidate
its hold on Iran up to the present border with the USSR.

Lord Curzon persuaded his colleagues in the war cabinet
that an agreement should be concluded with Iran that would
assure Britain a predominant position in that country. The

fruit of Curzon's maneuvering was the Anglo-Iranian Treaty of 1919, under which the British would have taken over the training of the Iranian army and would have organized the country's finances and the work of various key government departments. In effect, Britain would have established a veiled protectorate. The treaty was signed but never came into effect because the Majlis (parliament) refused to ratify it. Meanwhile, the last of the Qajars was overthrown, and Reza Khan seized power—he eventually came to rule as Reza Shah.

More important, the USSR reasserted its interest in Iranian affairs by invading Iran's Gilan province in May 1920, which, in effect, challenged British pretensions to hegemony south of the Caspian Sea. Had Britain wished, the situation might have reverted to what had prevailed in 1907, when Britain controlled southern Iran and Russia the north. But Britain did not want to return to that division, and the only remaining option was Lenczowski's third: a complete British withdrawal to the Gulf and a corresponding Russian withdrawal from Gilan, after which Iran would become nominally "independent . . . free from all foreign influences." This was the arrangement that finally transpired. Therefore the Russian invasion can be viewed as having ultimately benefited Iran, because it forced Britain to abandon its protectorate scheme.[2]

The USSR's changed relations with Iran freed the ruler of that country to begin earnestly to consolidate power in the central government. For Reza Shah, who was about to take power, the need to assert control was pressing because various peoples such as the Kurds, Lurs, Bakhtiaris, and Arabs of Mohammara were practically free agents. Further, they had thrived under the protection of the British practice of "second diplomacy," which meant that Britain, while carrying on normal diplomatic relations with Tehran, had dealt directly with tribal leaders, subsidizing them in many instances to ensure their cooperation. A move against any one of the leaders, therefore, would test whether Britain had in fact changed policy.

Mohammara was the chief city of the Iranian province that today is known as Khuzestan. Its shaikh was Arab, as indeed was a majority of the province's population. To the north of Mohammara lay the territory of the Bakhtiaris and the Lurs. The British had both the shaikh and the Bakhtiaris on permanent retainers, paying them 3 percent of the oil field revenues to keep them from puncturing the pipelines and otherwise disturbing the facilities.[3] Because the shaikh's lands spilled over into Iraq, the British upheld his claims there as well. Ernest Main describes the shaikh (who ultimately was knighted by the British: Shaikh Sir Khazal Khan) as something on the order of a medieval robber baron.[4]

In 1923, Reza Shah decided to reassert his country's suzerainty over the oil-rich Khuzestan area. This decision was a bold undertaking because he would have to not only confront the British but also transport his army to the region, which necessitated passing through rugged mountains that were the home of the Lurs and the Bakhtiaris, neither of whom was pacified. The first column the shah sent against the shaikh was ambushed by the Lurs,[5] lost over 100 men, and fled to Isfahan to the east. This rout convinced the shah that he must tend exclusively to the Lurs and subdue them before moving against the shaikh.

In 1924, Reza Shah tried again. He concentrated forces near Kermanshah, forced the mountain passes to the south, dispersed the Lurs, and reached the northern plain of Khuzestan at Dezful. In the autumn of that year, two army groups attacked Khuzestan and defeated the Bakhtiaris and the shaikh's forces. This operation underscored a point that would be made over and over again: Tribesmen without a friendly border at their back are no match for disciplined troops. To be sure, the shaikh had a friend in the British—and they held the mandate for Iraq, across whose border the shaikh might conveniently flee—but the British, it now became embarrassingly plain, could not preserve the shaikh and his lands in Iran.

The shaikh had an agreement of sorts with the British high commissioner in Mesopotamia, Sir Percy Cox, to which he attempted to hold the British.[6] Sir Percy told the shaikh that the agreement would not stand—indeed, could not do so. Against the pressing assault of a really determined Iranian ruler, the British had but one recourse if they were to thwart him—to introduce troops into the region—and circumstances militated against this action. As we have seen, any decisive British move in the south would have invited corresponding— and unacceptable—Russian moves in the north. This possibility of a Russian invasion had been reinforced by treaty because, as a consequence of withdrawing its troops from Gilan, the USSR had signed a friendship treaty with Iran in 1921 that empowered it to invade Iran if that country should be invaded by a third power. Unwilling to invite a direct confrontation with the USSR, Sir Percy counseled the shaikh to capitulate. He did so and was transported to Tehran, where he was confined to the city and a twenty-kilometer radius around it.[7]

At first glance, it appears the British came off badly, but although they lost face, they gained in the long run because their main requirement, a guarantee of stability, was assured.[8] Reza Shah was not anxious to disturb the Anglo-Persian Oil Company's operations, although later, when he renegotiated the company's concession, he drove a hard bargain. Under the old arrangement the company had witheld 16 percent of the royalties it paid the Iranian government to compensate for the protection money it had to pay to the local chiefs. However, the shah insisted that the money be remitted to him now that his troops protected the fields.[9] For the tribesmen with the wit to appreciate it, a warning had been given. Reza Shah would now, in effect, control the border region, at least in the west, and subdue the tribes relentlessly.

By 1929, only one unpacified region remained, and it was to the south and southwest of Isfahan. Here were the important non-Kurdish tribes of the Bakhtiaris and Qashqai, all well armed with weapons smuggled to them by the gun-running shaikhs of the Trucial Coast. These tribes started a general revolt, but it, too, was quelled, comparatively bloodlessly. The Bakhtiari's were bought off by the Iranian government's essentially taking over the subsidy payments of the British.

Ernest Main refers to humiliations suffered by Great Britain at the hands of Reza Shah, and he claims that the shah's aggressive policy was encouraged by Britain's policy of conciliation. This claim may be true, but it is also true that at no time did Reza Shah's policy seriously endanger Britain's vital interests. Temperley says that Britain's interest in the Gulf oil fields was "naval therefore vital." Britain gave in on a great many issues in its conflict with Iran, but whenever the vital matter of oil arose, Britain's response invariably was quick and energetic.

When Iran reasserted a claim to the island of Bahrain (strategically situated in the Gulf) in 1927, the British tied the matter up in the world court in the Hague. (At the outbreak of World War II, when Reza was deposed by the Allies, the matter still had not been resolved.)[10] Again, when Reza canceled the Anglo-Persian Oil Company's concession in 1932, claiming insufficient royalties, Britain sent naval vessels into the Gulf and threatened to use force if necessary. The concession was renegotiated to the satisfaction of both parties, which would seem to indicate that as long as the Iranians did not interfere with the production of oil and were willing to accept the royalties that Britain agreed to pay them, Britain had no urgent requirement to physically possess the oil region. The policy Britain pursued toward the tribes could, then, have been easily dispensed with. I stress this point because we shall shortly see that Britain made similar accommodations with the Iraqi government, but at the expense of the Assyrian and Kurdish tribes.

By the early 1930s, Iran had pacified that country's tribes. Some, such as the Kurdish Fayalis, suffered grievously in the process, being driven off their lands into permanent exile in Iraq. But most were merely disarmed and the nomads were settled on the land; in many cases an arrangement was made whereby a few tribesmen were allowed to take the flocks to the traditional high pastures—under a guard of gendarmes.[11] Reza experimented with forcing the Kurds to abandon their traditional costume (the Iranians subsequently relented on this point) and he moved the tribal chiefs off the land—some were compelled to live in areas far from their homes; others, in Tehran. At no point, however, did the shah try to force cultural assimilation on the Kurds, which was a feature of Turkish policy.

Turkey

The Turks, like the Iranians under Reza Shah, were somewhat free of big-power constraints after World War I, but the Turkish situation differed in several significant respects from the Iranian. In Iran oil proved the salvation of the state: With proceeds from the sale of oil, the Iranian government raised and equipped an army and subdued all the recalcitrant elements. Turkey, on the other hand, already had an army, one that had taken it through World War I. Although the Turkish army had been defeated, not all of its units had been ineffective; some had been quite formidable. But Turkey had no oil and its economic situation was desperate; unexpectedly, the Soviet Union came to its aid by providing the Kemalists with arms and ammunition. With this aid, the Turks dispatched the Armenians and the Greeks and crushed the rebellion of Shaikh Said in 1925. Armies in both Iran and Turkey, then, laid the foundation of aggressive nationalism, but in the case of Turkey, unification was not at all easy. The Iranians, in fact, were a minority in their own "empire," but there were so many minorities that none stood out. Such was not the case in Turkey, where there was only one real minority group, the Kurds, and they constituted perhaps one-fifth of the total population. As we have seen, they had long been a source of trouble for the Turks, most recently at the time of Shaikh Said's great revolt in 1925.

The expressions of Kurdish nationalism that accompanied a few of the earlier risings were largely pro forma; more often, no connection was made between a particular rising and ambitions for a Kurdish nation state. After the 1925 revolt, this situation changed, and increasingly, nationalism was ascribed as a motive for Kurdish agitation. The problem is to discover whether the nationalist motive actually existed at the time or was grafted onto the revolts after the fact. It was the fashion in those days—and, indeed, today—to do everything in the name of national self-determination, so one is not surprised that the 1930 revolt of Ihsan Nuri and the 1937 revolt in Dersim northeast of Diyarbakir are presented in much of the literature as calculated nationalist risings.[12] On the other hand, the Turks carried out fierce repressions after the Shaikh Said revolt—the sort a fledgling regime that was still not fully established would resort to in order to achieve security. Those measures, which included forced transportation and all the other extreme actions detailed in Chapter 3, intensified Kurdish antagonisms. As Turkey's economic priorities began to have effect, making the lot of the Kurds harder and harder, one would naturally expect eruptions. The question is whether the Turks goaded the Kurds into violence with their economic and cultural reforms or whether the Kurdish nationalists contrived and organized the rebellion.

The Kurdish writers Soreya Badr Khan, Kendal (pseud.), and Abdur Rahman Ghassemlou credit the patriotic Kurdish organization Hoyboon with instigating the Kurdish revolts of the 1930s. Hoyboon was the progenitor of the Kurdish Democratic party and of the Komola, which came into existence after World War II.

In effect, Hoyboon was the first organized expression of exclusively nationalistic sentiment among the Kurds. Its origins are obscure, but there are even hints that it was instigated by the British, either alone or in conjunction with the French.[13] The group's first convention was held in Bihamdun, Lebanon, in 1927, and the founding members—all of them former landowning aristocrats of Kurdistan—included such notables as Prince Kiamuran Bedr Khan, Memduh Selim Bey, Shahin Bey, and Ihsan Nuri Pasha, who was named commander of the Kurdish army. Early in its existence, Hoyboon had close links to the Armenian community, which may at first seem anomalous since the two communities had a history of deep enmity dating from the days of Abdul Hamid. Nevertheless, V. Papaziian, leader of the Armenian Dashnakyans (a nationalist organization), attended the first convention of Hoyboon,[14] so it may have been the Armenians, not the British, who were instrumental in forming the organization.

The Armenians had lost a great deal after World War I— after seeming to have made great gains—when the Turks and the Russians joined forces and crushed the Armenian republic. Moreover, the Turks had driven most of the Armenians out of their traditional homeland in central and northeastern Anatolia, and Kurds had moved in. The association of Armenians and Kurds in Hoyboon seems, then, to have been a convenient merger. The Armenians provided money, organizational skills, and contacts with Western European countries that might be expected to espouse the rebels' cause against the Turks;[15] the Kurds supplied the fighting force. Since vast areas of Armenia and Kurdistan overlap, presumably a condominium form of rule would have been worked out if the rebels had been successful.

The great rising of the 1930s began on June 20, 1930, with the revolt of Kurds of the Jelali tribe, which lived on both sides of the Turko-Iranian border around Mount Ararat. After the revolt had started, Ihsan Nuri, a nationalist (and also an officer in the Turkish army who had fought in the war against the Greeks), took charge. Other tribes joined in—although Arfa notes that in some places the population, supported by frontier guards and gendarmes, resisted.[16] The Turks responded by massing 12,000 men between Van and Igdir near the Soviet border and then moving east. Meanwhile, the rebels were trying to penetrate the region of the 1925 revolt as they hoped to enlist the support of the Kurds there who had been victims of Turkish repression. The Turks quickly checked the rebellion's spread and drove the rebels back toward the Iranian border.

Immediately, the Turkish government protested to Iran about permitting the Kurds to cross the border. Although the Iranian government proved cooperative in this instance, the Turks insisted on an adjustment of the border that would bring all of Mount Ararat and the Jelali Kurds under their control. (The agreement was arrived at in 1932, the Turks giving in exchange the same amount of territory in the area west of the Rezaiyeh.)

The Kurds' intention was to make a stand on Mount Ararat, but the Turks brought in aircraft to strafe the Kurds' encampments. The revolt was two months old when Kurdish chiefs from the French-mandated territory of Syria attempted to cross that border to aid the Turkish Kurds. The Syrian Kurds were easily driven back by the Turks, and the revolt was over. However, the attempt is significant in that it was the first "sign of co-operation between Kurdish elements not related to one another by local or personal interests."[17]

After the revolt of Ihsan Nuri and the Jelalis, Turkey's harsh repressions were renewed. It is hard to evaluate the claims of the nationalists, such as those found in Kendal that up to 1 million Kurds were displaced, the inhabitants of whole villages being moved in forced marches across the plains of Anatolia in winter.[18] Kendal claims that "only a shortage of material means prevented the Ankara government from deporting the whole Kurdish population."[19] Ghassemlou refers to a new law passed by Turkey in 1932 whereby "hundreds of thousands of Kurds were deported into areas where they were to constitute five percent of the population."[20] According to Arshak Safrastian, "the depopulation and devastation of the provinces east of the Euphrates, begun in 1915 by the murder and spoliation of the Armenians, was nearly completed during 1925–32 by the murder and spoliation of the Kurds."[21] These writers are all Kurdish nationalists or sympathizers. Minorsky, though, says that "since the settlement of the Mosul question (1926), the Ankara government has enforced a policy the tendency of which is to eliminate from Kurdistan feudal and tribal influences."[22] There appears to be no question that a policy of Turkification, or assimilation, was pursued. Its scope and dimensions (in terms of casualties cited by the extreme Kurdish nationalists) may perhaps be questioned.

The Turks were pushing further and further into Kurdistan, establishing gendarmerie posts in the remotest regions. In June 1937, when they tried to set up posts in Dersim, they encountered opposition from Dersim chiefs, who had not yet been touched by the Turkification policy. A chief of the Kurdish Abbasushaghi tribe, Sayyid Reza, gathered a force of a few thousand fighters of various tribes, attacked the posts, and drove off the gendarmes. After the entire Dersim district had fallen to the Kurds, the Turks ringed it with troops. Again the Kurds' strategy was to hold out in the high mountains of the region, but once more the superior military machine of the Turks proved effective. On November 14, 1937, Shaikh Sayyid Reza, his two sons, and some other chiefs were tried, condemned, and executed.

Arfa claims the Turkish government ordered the deportation of all the Kurdish clans that had participated in the revolt—some 90,000 persons—to other *wilayets*.[23] Thus, as of 1937, the situation of the Kurds in Turkey was dismal indeed. Their tribal society was being torn apart, and their very identity—down to the way they dressed—was being denied them. Instead of their traditional clothing, which was so sensible for the region—the spacious pantaloons, embroidered stomachers, and turbans—they were compelled to assume "modern" dress, the drab outfit of the city-bred Turk. Interestingly, though, the Kurds are even now not wholly assimilated. The Turkish government, lacking the money to develop the whole country evenly, has continued to favor the western lands of Anatolia. This policy has had the effect of leaving the Kurds somewhat alone—sunken in their poverty, certainly, but nevertheless still an element that is set apart from the rest of Turkish society. And, as we shall see, this situation has resulted in a potentially dangerous state of affairs.

Iraq

We might say that in 1930–1937, a vise was closing on the Kurds—at least in Turkey and Iran. In Iraq the Kurds were somewhat freer, but their tribal society had all but disappeared as a result of the British policy of aggrandizing the *agha*s and beys.

Detribalization

Methods of imperial control differ. For example, the French actively promoted ethnic diversity in the areas of the Middle East that they took over; the British preferred to bolster the ruling class.[24] Thus, in Iraq, the British arranged matters so there would be a dependent class of shaikhs, *agha*s, and beys, and they so structured society that the promotion of these people was ensured. As early as 1918, the British had enacted regulations concerning tribal disputes, which had the effect of setting up a two-tiered system of justice[25] under which the central government could not interfere with the administration of tribal justice: The tribesmen and *miskīn* in the north and the landless Arab tenants in the south were subject to tribal law.

The British further encouraged policies that bound the landless Arab tenants to the land of the shaikh or Kurdish *agha*s or beys. In 1932, the British supported the Iraqi monarchy in sponsoring legislation that extended the land policies of the Turks. The Turkish *tapu,* the category of land-holding introduced in 1858, had represented the beginning of private property ownership, and tribal leaders such as the Barzinjas had taken advantage of it to get tribal lands registered as their personal property. The new category of land promoted by the British was known as *lazmah;* it was, in effect, an extention of private property, and it, too, was exploited by the tribal leaders.

The transformation of the tribal leaders from tribute-receiving princes (which they were during the period when the

Babans were in control) to simple landlords took about half a century. In the end, the leading tribal figures had only the barest connection with their tribes. They did not, by the time of the British, even act as go-betweens, for Britain sponsored changes that required that administrators in the Kurdish area speak Kurdish, and the lower classes—the tribesmen, *miskīn,* and migrant laborers—could henceforth deal with the central government directly. The tribal leaders had also lost their former position as war leaders; their power was now exclusively based on the possession of land.

Some of the leaders (and this was true of the Kurds) became extraordinarily wealthy. Batatu gives statistics that show that the beys of the Jaf tribe in 1958 owned 539,333 *dunum*s surrounding as-Sulaymaniyah, Kirkuk, and Dizalah.[26] He also breaks down the major landlords into religious and ethnic categories: In 1958, of a total of forty-nine Iraqi families owning more than 30,000 *dunum*s, eleven were Kurds.[27] To be sure, not all of the erstwhile *agha*s and beys of Iraqi Kurdistan became plutocrats under the British, but all did experience an appreciable rise in status.

Obviously, there was method in the British policy toward the tribal leaders. Immediately after World War I, the leaders, and hence the tribes, had been hostile toward the central government, but as the tribal leaders became more and more wealthy by becoming landowners, they began to identify their interests with those of the ruling family—and against those of the army, which represented the interests of the emerging Iraqi middle class.[28]

Under successive governments tribal leaders composed significant blocks of the parliamentary membership. In 1924, of ninety-nine members of the Iraqi Constituent Assembly, thirty-four were shaikhs, *agha*s, or beys, and some of these were Kurds.[29] Hamid Bey of the Jaf tribe belonged to the higher directorate of Nuri as-Said's Constitutional Union Party,[30] and the Babans regularly assumed portfolios under Nuri. This increasing involvement of the tribal leaders in government may explain the comparatively quiescent behavior of the Kurds in Iraq, whereas all around—in Turkey and Iran—they were in open revolt.[31]

Another reason the tribal leaders were motivated to support the monarchy was that they were lightly taxed.[32] Batatu says that in 1911, revenue from land composed 44.3 percent of all state receipts; in 1919, it yielded only about 30 percent, and the bulk of that sum was derived from taxes on townsmen[33]— shaikhs and *agha*s were immune from taxes.

With the exception of Shaikh Mahmud (who, in his behavior, was something of a throwback), Kurdish leaders gave the central government little trouble during the period up to World War II. They were wealthier under the British and the monarchy than most of them had a right to expect, and they had a status as members of the Constituent Assembly. What they lacked—although this situation was disguised—was power. Their true power base was the tribes, but their relationship to the tribes had been undermined.[34] The tribal leaders–cum–landlords had moved to Baghdad in order to protect their interests by being closer to the seat of government, and soon they did not dare return to their "estates" because their erstwhile tribesmen—once they appreciated the trick played on them by the *lazmah* enactments—had turned vengeful.

In the late 1930s, the transformation of the tribal leaders was complete, and the countryside of Iraq was effectively tied into the British imperial market. The growth of river traffic on the Tigris had promoted a market economy over vast stretches of Iraq so that land that had been given over to subsistence agriculture was now devoted to the production of the cash crops of wheat, rice, and tobacco.[35] This change benefited the erstwhile tribal leaders, who had gone from being nomad warriors to tribute-receiving lords and tax farmers under the later Ottomans, then landlords. They were now owners of huge estates and exploiters of their former tribesmen, who were now their tenant farmers. Thus, though the Kurds in Iraq did not suffer oppression such as the Kurds in Iran and Turkey did, they were nevertheless effectively detribalized. In addition, even as early as 1932, one event should have given the Iraqi Kurds a warning of future troubles. The massacre of Assyrians at Simel and their desertion by the British, behavior that echoed Britain's betrayal of the shaikh of Mohammara, meant that the British would not stand by their assurances to the League of Nations that they would guarantee the rights of the minorities in Iraq.

The Simel Massacre

In 1931, the outstanding minority problems in Iraq concerned the Kurds and Assyrians (the Iraqis had previously settled matters concerning their Jewish and Armenian communities).[36] The Assyrians claimed the protection of the Church of England and therefore, apparently assuming the British were in Iraq to stay, wanted no formal guarantees. The Kurds, being Sunni Muslims, were on their own, but in 1932, they had no reason to believe that they could not defend themselves against an untried and apparently inept Iraqi army.

The Assyrians' assumption that they were safe because they had British backing was mistaken, and yet there was every reason why they should have made it. Assyrian levies (mercenaries) had been incorporated into Britain's defense force in Iraq: They not only guarded the RAF base at Habbaniya west of Baghdad, but they also were sent to subdue Euphrates and Kurdish tribesmen. Still, as in the cases of Turkey and Iran, Britain faced diminution of its control over Iraq, as its increasing reliance on the RAF showed. As in Iran, Britain required a stable regime in Iraq, one that could be counted on not to obstruct Britain's vital interests. The British were willing to ensure these conditions by supporting the central government of Iraq—and, in effect, traded short-term diplomatic concessions for long-term stability.

Compromises were struck in a series of treaties and League of Nations decisions between 1922 and 1932. Britain agreed in 1922—under pressure from Iraqi nationalists—to exercise its control in Iraq by means of a treaty instead of a formal mandate. This treaty was to run for four years. However, the

League of Nations commission felt that the rights of minorities in Iraq must be safeguarded, and therefore the League of Nations agreed to Iraq's annexation of Mosul in 1926 only if Iraq and Great Britain concluded a treaty guaranteeing a British presence in Iraq for twenty-five years. In 1930, a new Anglo-Iraqi treaty, which included the twenty-five-year provision, was signed, but it made no mention of minority rights, which gave the Assyrians and Kurds pause.

The Kurdish and Assyrian communities reacted forcefully, and the rights question was raised in the Iraqi parliament by six Kurdish deputies. Earlier, these same six deputies had presented a petition to that body demanding, one, increased expenditure for education; two, the formation of a special Kurdish administrative unit (to be governed by a Kurdish inspector-general who was to be the sole link between the area and the central government) composed of the *liwa*s of as-Sulaymaniyah, Irbil, and Kirkuk and a new *liwa* to be formed from the Kurdish areas of the Mosul *liwa;* and, three, increased expenditures for public services in the Kurdish areas. Nothing had come of these demands because the Baghdad government had felt that to accede to them would encourage further separatist tendencies. Disturbances erupted in the Kurdish districts, with the worst being in as-Sulaymaniyah where thirteen fatalities were recorded. Then, in September 1930, Shaikh Mahmud slipped across the border from Iran where he had been in exile, demanded a British mandate for Kurdistan, and continued in rebellion for a year.

The Kurdish agitation seems to have been quite forceful (although in the end, nothing came of it), but the Assyrian reaction was much more extreme, and once again, a great tragedy was enacted. The account of the Simel massacre has to be given in some detail if the behavior of the British is to be fully appreciated.[37]

Immediately after hearing of the British-Iraqi treaty arrangements, the Assyrians, led by their patriarch the Mar Shimoun, adopted a truculent stance. They demanded land and insisted on being settled all in one unit, stating baldly that should the Iraqi government prove dilatory in meeting their demands, they would seize the land they coveted, *in Mosul.* Clearly, the Assyrians counted on the backing of the British and, perhaps more crucially, of the Church of England, for it was the British who had brought them to Iraq as refugees after the Turks had driven them from eastern Anatolia. In responding to the Assyrians, the Iraqi government took a similarly unyielding position. The Iraqis insisted that they truly intended to settle the Assyrians but they despaired of finding enough tillable land to settle them as one unit. Further, the Iraqis demanded that before arrangements for settlement proceeded, the Mar Shimoun must publicly renounce his temporal authority.

In 1933, an armed party of some 500 Assyrians, led by Yacu, a commander of the Iraqi levies, crossed the border into French-mandated Syria. Survivors later revealed that they had been led by the Mar Shimoun to believe that land awaited them there, but they soon saw that there was no such land. When the Assyrians sought to return, the Iraqi army met them at the Tigris River and would not permit them to return unless they laid down their arms. Neither side won the ensuing pitched battle, but the stalemate was, in effect, a victory for the Iraqi army as it had had a poor reputation and had been scorned by the tough Assyrian mountaineers.

As the Assyrians moved off the field, word spread of the engagement, and in the mountains beyond the Tigris, the Assyrian villagers who had been left behind when Yacu's party had crossed into Syria began to prepare for trouble. At Simel, near Tall 'Afar, Assyrian men, women, and children were induced by the Iraqi gendarmes to surrender themselves to the protection of the police. They did so, but the Iraqi police then connived, apparently with elements of the army, to brutally massacre these unfortunates.[38] The death toll was later set at 600.

Before examining the causes of this massacre, we should note what did not happen, namely, Britain made no effective protest. The Simel massacre might have provided all the excuse the British needed to defy Iraqi nationalism by reoccupying the country, but they did not do so, probably because British interests would not have been served by such a move. Toynbee writes:

> The British Government did, in fact, very quickly make up their mind not merely to refrain from any intervention in Iraq on their own part, but also to assist the Iraqi Government to put the best possible face upon the situation at Geneva; and it seems probable that, in coming to this decision, British statesmen were actuated by other motives besides an anxiety to avoid precipitating further massacres of the Assyrian and other Christian minorities in the Mosul wilayet. Both the British Government and certain powerful British business concerns had interests in Iraq which they were eager to preserve. The Government wished to maintain the airbases on Iraqi territory which were links in the chain of the military and commercial air route from Great Britain to India and Australia; the Iraq Petroleum Company wanted to enjoy the benefit of the concession which it had received from the Iraqi Government. In the nineteenth century, such considerations might have led a British Government to jump at the pretext offered by the Simel massacre for reversing the policy of 1929, and perhaps even the policy of 1920, and virtually annexing Iraq to the British Empire; but this form of Imperialism ... required the employment of military force; and in 1933 this force was not at the British Government's command; for the British voter and taxpayer ... no longer saw any glamour in the exercise of political dominion over Oriental countries; and he [the British voter] had only acquiesced in the British Government's assumption of mandatory responsibilities in Iraq on the tacit understanding that these responsibilities should be liquidated at the earliest opportunity and, in the meantime, should involve the Government's constituents in the United Kingdom in no appreciable liabilities, either military, political or financial.[39]

Accordingly, one would have to conclude that the massacre of 600 Assyrians did not constitute instability in British eyes (the definition of instability would have to be anything that threatened British interests). Indeed, the incident could be shown to have ameliorated the British position in Iraq because the Assyrians were proving an awkward liability. They had earned the intense hatred of the Kurds by their connection with the British defense force in Iraq, they had been openly scornful of the Iraqi army, and they had been bent on seizing territory from the sovereign government of Iraq—all of which they could not have done without British support. Whatever the extenuating circumstances for the British behavior, one fact was now proved: Britain's abandonment of the shaikh of Mohammara was not an isolated reaction, but part of British policy.

The most convincing explanation of why the Simel massacre occurred at all is offered by Toynbee, and his comments illuminate the Kurds' situation as well.[40] Toynbee says that a crisis of tribal authority was occurring. During the Ottoman Empire period, the religious leaders of protected minorities had exercised temporal authority, but after World War I and the dissolution of the empire, that authority was claimed by national leaders. The situation of the Assyrians may be considered an extreme example of how the spiritual-temporal authority operated. In corresponding with the Iraqi authorities, the Mar Shimoun wrote:

This Patriarchal authority is a great historical and traditional usage of the Assyrian people and Church, and it has been one of the established and most important customs. The temporal power has not been assumed by me, but it has descended to me from centuries past as a legalized delegation of the people to the Patriarch. It was not only tolerated but also officially recognized in past by the old Sasanid Kings, Islamic Caliphs, Moghul Khans and Ottoman Sultans. No proof of any misuse of this power, as far as any King or Government whose subjects the Assyrian people have been, can be traced in history, whilst on the other hand, besides being in no way preventive to the application of the law of the country, it has proved to be the best method of dealing with a people living under the circumstances as the Assyrians are. Under the above circumstances I very much regret to say that it is impossible for me to comply with your order—viz. to sign the written promise outlined by Your Excellency—since such an action would only mean that I am willingly withdrawing myself from the duty to my people: the duty which, as mentioned above, is a legal delegation of the people to me and it is only to them to take it away.[41]

Thus the Assyrians' subsequent flouting of the wishes of the Iraqi central government can be read as support of their traditional religious leader against the claims of a new—and as yet unestablished—secular, national authority. It was a test in which neither side could give way. To do so would have meant, on the Assyrian side, a fundamental altering of communal relationships; on the Iraqi side, it would have meant an undermining of the new government's claim to rule.

The Kurds' experience was similar to that of the Assyrians. With detribalization and the collapse of the old Kurdish war machine—that is, the confederacy of warring tribes led by a paramount chief—only one mobilizing agent remained, the religious shaikhs with their appeal to the faith. These shaikhs tried to step into the power vacuum left by the departed princely rulers. The shaikhs flourished for a while, but then they were cut down by the onslaught of nationalism. The reason they resisted so stubbornly, not to say quixotically, was that the challenge posed by nationalism threatened the very basis of Kurdish society.

Regional Cooperation and Kurdish Nationalism

In addition to the consolidating policies of the young nation states, one other significant change affected the fortunes of the Kurds in the 1930s, the introduction of the concept of regional stability guaranteed by regional alliances. In 1921 (and again in 1928), the USSR had worked out a series of treaties that allied that country with Turkey, Iran, and Afghanistan and those states with each other. These alliances not only assured the USSR of peace to the south, but also, by inducing the three countries to develop mechanisms for settling quarrels among themselves, ensured that meddling foreign powers (like Great Britain) could not find pretexts to intervene in the region.

However, as Toynbee notes, the Soviet Union's "good neighbor policy" to the south ultimately foundered.[42] As the USSR's economic problems persisted into the 1930s, that government was forced to take steps that aggravated distressing economic conditions in the countries to the south. Another development to upset conditions in these countries was that fascist Italy had begun to be a power in the eastern Mediterranean and countries like Turkey and Iraq had begun to fear Italian expansionist designs. These twin factors induced the countries of the area to cooperate. In 1937, they cobbled together the Saadabad Pact, which encouraged cooperation between Iran, Iraq, and Turkey. A key provision was Article 7, which inveighed against the "formation and activity of associations, organizations, or armed bands seeking to overthrow established institutions."[43]

Kurdish nationalists profess that this article was directed against them, and one can sympathize with that view. Anything that facilitated cooperation among the regional powers and diminished their mutual hostility and suspicion promoted regional stability—a desideratum for Britain and the USSR. Regional alliances also had the effect of institutionalizing stability, and stability worked against the interest of the nationalist-minded Kurds. We shall see in the next chapter how World War II disrupted security arrangements in the area. With the superpowers' attention turned toward Europe and fighting the Axis powers, the Kurdish tribes erupted again, and the recently achieved regional stability vanished.

5
The Kurdish Republic and Russian Involvement

The Kurds' methods of guerrilla campaigning are nowhere systematically discussed, and even the allusions that do exist must be ferreted out. When studied, these methods show considerable coherence and are sensibly practical. The basic principle is economy of effort: maximum commitment when a battle turns in one's favor; unrestrained flight when disaster threatens; and if neither flight nor fighting seems advisable, total submission. The tribes never fight—at least not effectively—more than a tribe's length from their home territory,[1] and they do not remain in the field unless there is a continuing prospect of loot. Under the Ottomans it was a rule that tribes fighting tribes never destroyed fixed property.

All these restrictions would seem to support the assumption that for the Kurds, fighting used to be a practical business. One fought to preserve the honor of the tribe; one fought for loot; one fought to fill a power vacuum whenever one might appear. One did not fight for reasons of imperialist aggression. The Kurds seem to be one of those peoples of modern history who, while conscious of their corporate identity, would not ordinarily think it worthwhile to develop any nationalist commitment. It was not until relatively late (halfway through World War II) that societal changes in the countries where the Kurds dwelt forced them to develop at least a defensive nationalism.[2]

The significant change in the Kurds' attitude toward controlling "their" land came in the 1940s when the Mahabad Republic was founded, and most authorities date the beginning of an authentic Kurdish national movement from this period. This development came about because whatever was holding the Kurds back (be it geography, cultural backwardness, or other factors), that factor or factors no longer effectively outweighed the major threat that confronted the Kurds. In the era of nationalism, there were no rules of warfare by which the Kurds could protect themselves. After the actions of Ataturk in Turkey, those of Reza Shah in Iran, and the detribalization resulting from British policy in Iraq, Kurds everywhere faced the choice of assimilating or being eliminated. The creation of the Mahabad Republic was therefore a healthy Kurdish response to a lethal threat.

The Russians have a long history of association—not always a congenial one—with the fortunes of the Kurds. However, their sponsorship of the Mahabad Republic in Iran was a landmark in that history. But before dealing with this involvement, we must examine developments in Iraq that were to have a bearing on the setting up of the new republic.

The Barzanis

By World War II, the majority of the Kurdish tribes in Iraq existed on paper only. The tribesmen were no longer freeholders; the tribal leaders were in most cases living apart from the tribes in Baghdad or as-Sulaymaniyah. The only area in which the old ways prevailed, which Fredrik Barth calls "tribal organization,"[3] was in the far northeastern corner of Iraq, the most inaccessible area of the country and the home of the Barzanis. The tribal history of this particular group is comparatively short. The Barzani tribe was formed in the early part of the nineteenth century when adherents of other tribes associated themselves with the first shaikh of Barzan, Taj ad Din, a Sufi who had received his patent from Maulana Khalid, a leader of the Naqshbandi order,[4] and whose piety and miracle-working reputation won him a large following.[5] The tribe originally numbered only 750 families,[6] but as more and more Kurds devoted themselves to the shaikh of Barzan, the tribe grew. Soon whole tribes had made their submission: the Shirwan (1,800 families in 1906), the Mizuri (120 families), and the small Dola Mari. In 1945, the followers of the shaikh of Barzan had stabilized at about 1,800 families, or 9,000 people.[7]

During and after World War II, Shaikh Ahmad led the tribe along with his younger brother, Mulla Mustafa. To the world, Mulla Mustafa was preeminent, but he himself deferred to his brother Ahmad who was an eccentric (a characteristic of Kurdish Sufis, Edmonds claims).[8] One report states that the Barzanis had their first significant brush with the Iraq authorities in 1927 because Ahmad had fallen into heresy, sanctioning the consumption of pork by his followers and espousing several other practices repugnant to good Muslims.[9] His "error" is supposed to have provoked an attack against him by the Bardost tribe. Four years later, Ahmad revolted over a plan to settle Assyrians in his tribal area.[10] The Iraqi army sent two columns against him but was defeated, largely because of the fighting skills of Mulla Mustafa. Eventually, the RAF bombed Ahmad, Mulla Mustafa, and their followers, and they fled to Turkey. The Turks in this instance cooperated with the Iraqis and captured and handed the Barzanis over to the authorities in Baghdad. The two brothers then experienced a decade of exile, first in southern Iraq, then in as-Sulaymaniyah.

We have no record of how the Barzanis spent their time in as-Sulaymaniyah, but we do know they barely survived on the meager allowance given them.[11] As-Sulaymaniyah was then—and is to this day—the cultural and revolutionary capital of Kurdistan,[12] and we must assume that Mulla Mustafa absorbed some of the teachings of Kurdish nationalist intellectuals there; otherwise his subsequent career as a nationalist would not make sense. In 1943, after selling his wife's gold ornaments to augment his income,[13] Mulla Mustafa and a few followers left as-Sulaymaniyah and, traveling by way of Iran, secretly returned to Barzan. Although he is supposed to have given his pledge to keep the peace, it was not long before he had provoked Iraq's central government.

It is not apparent what the exact character of his trouble-making was. There are writers, Arfa among them, who claim that Mulla Mustafa immediately launched a full-scale revolt for Kurdish autonomy in the Barzan region[14] and that Prime Minister Nuri as-Said was persuaded by the British to negotiate with him. A representative, a Kurd loyal to the Iraqi government, was sent north to open negotiations between Mulla Mustafa and Baghdad on the basis of a list of nationalist demands. Another version ascribes the revolt to the usual tribal politics and states that Mulla Mustafa set out on his return to recoup his tribe's diminished fortunes, which could come only at the expense of the Zibaris, the Bardost tribe, and the other Barzani enemies.[15]

There is a hint in the histories that the British intrigued with Mulla Mustafa to set him against Baghdad.[16] Again, as with so many events having to do with the Kurds, the timing of the revolt is suspect. In 1941, Iraq had weathered a short-lived nationalist coup by army officers, which had forced Abdul Ilah (the regent), Nuri as-Said, and a majority of the cabinet officers loyal to Britain to flee to Transjordan. The British had put down this rebellion by force of arms, and by 1942, the regent, Nuri, and the supporters of Britain had been reinstalled. Still, nationalists in the Iraqi army remained unreconciled, and Mulla Mustafa's revolt in 1943 mainly discomfited the Iraqi army.

After the nationalists in Nuri's cabinet balked at conceding to Barzani's demands, there were continued negotiations. But in August 1945, Mulla Mustafa responded to a provocative attack, and the Iraqi army advanced toward Barzan; Mulla Mustafa ordered his men, a force of about 4,000 or 5,000, to resist. The Iraqi force of some 30,000 soldiers,[17] supplemented by Kurdish units from tribes hostile to the Barzanis, began to close in on Mulla Mustafa and his brother (who had earlier been allowed to return to Barzan). The Barzanis fought doggedly and well—late in August, Mulla Mustafa badly mauled the Iraqi Fifth Brigade, which he had trapped in ambush. However, the combined assault against the Barzanis proved too much, and the brothers ordered a general retreat—not merely of the fighting tribesmen, but of the entire tribe. In September 1945, some 10,000 Barzanis (among them 3,000 fighters)[18] crossed the border into Iran and offered their arms to the newly proclaimed Mahabad Republic in return for maintenance.

This sudden appearance of the Barzanis on the border of Mahabad has to be viewed as an event of considerable significance. That one of the most primitive of the Kurdish tribes would be dislodged from its protective surroundings is hardly extraordinary—since Turks and Iranians were continually uprooting Kurdish tribes at that time—but the fact that the tribe could move intact and armed, executing an orderly retreat, was less usual. And now the tribe was offering its services to the leaders of the Mahabad Republic.

Mahabad, Azerbaijan, and the USSR

Russian involvement with the Kurds goes back at least to czarist times, when the Russians incurred the Kurds' deep resentment by supporting Armenian nationalist claims to lands that were largely shared with the Kurds. Nevertheless, so many Kurds so close to the border of the Soviet Union could not be ignored, and under certain conditions the USSR cultivated them.[19] In 1923, when the khan of Maku revolted against Iran, the Russians accredited a consul to the khanate,[20] and in 1927, they established a GPU (Gosudarstvennoye Politcheskoye Upravleniye) resident in Mahabad to conduct propaganda activity.[21] In 1942, when the German armies were slashing south and east into the Caucasus, the Russians convened an impromptu conference of Kurdish leaders at Baku and asked for Kurdish-Russian amity before the Axis onslaught.

But in order to understand how the Russians came to be involved with the Kurds of Mahabad, we must refer to the geopolitical analysis presented earlier. As we have seen, at the end of World War I, Britain hoped to benefit from the success of the Bolshevik revolution by turning all of Iran into a protectorate. However, the Soviets acted decisively by introducing troops into northern Iran and, in effect, laying down a challenge: The country should be divided into separate British and Russian spheres of interest. Britain did not want such a division, so a more congenial arrangement was arrived at: Britain backed off to the Gulf, and Russian troops withdrew to the Soviet Union. The situation in Iran after World War II was the same except that the roles of the main protagonists were reversed. This time, it was Great Britain that appeared incapable of fulfilling its imperial obligations, and the Soviet Union, apparently in consequence of this fact, pressed an aggressive policy. Specifically, Britain and the USSR had been in Iran under a tripartite treaty with that country. During the war, Iran had been occupied by Britain and the USSR to facilitate the flow of materials from the West to the Soviet Union through the Gulf and overland to the Caspian Sea. The treaty provided that Britain and the USSR would evacuate their forces from Iran six months after the defeat of Germany or its allies. Japan capitulated on September 2, 1945, and on January 1, 1946, Britain departed. The Russians stayed on. In the meantime, in November 1945, there had been a revolt in the province of Azerbaijan in northwestern Iran, and an Azerbaijan Republic had been set up under the protection of the Red army. An attempt by the shah to reoccupy Azerbaijan was balked by the Russians, and the matter hung fire while British, American, and Russian diplomats negotiated.

The British first set forth a scheme that would, in effect, have certified the changed realities.[22] They proposed that Azerbaijan claim autonomy within Iran and that similar arrangements be worked out for Iranian Kurdistan, Khuzestan, and other areas. According to this plan, Iran would have lost control over its ethnic groups and would have, in effect, reverted to its condition in 1907, when the Anglo-Russian Treaty had divided Persia into Russian and British spheres of interest. The Russians seem to have considered Britain's proposal only briefly before they rejected it, believing, according to Arfa, that they could have both northern and southern provinces.[23]

The Soviet Union's concern was with Azerbaijan, but another separatist state emerged in Iran at the end of World War II: the Mahabad Republic. Although the Azerbaijan Republic was instigated by the Russians, the Mahabad Republic was more likely created by default, to judge from the manner in which the Kurds brought their minute republic into being. The Russian sphere in Iran, according to the tripartite treaty, clearly included the province of Azerbaijan, just as the British one included southern Kurdistan. But northern Kurdistan, the area around Mahabad, fell between the two spheres. Once the Azerbaijanis proclaimed their separatist scheme, with Russian support, the problem of what to do with the northern Kurds arose. Britain could not move north to include them in the British sphere, and initially, the Russians ignored them. The Mahabad Kurds, led by a religious figure, Qazi Moham-mad, took the opportunity and on their own initiative declared their independence.

When the Kurds first approached the Russians for support in founding the Mahabad Republic, the Russians demurred, suggesting that the Kurds associate with their fellow strugglers in Azerbaijan. To the Kurds, the Azerbaijanis not only were Turks, but also were of an entirely different level of culture and sophistication. The Azerbaijan were townsmen by and large, and the Kurds were rural: Of the 40,000 families that eventually came to be encompassed within the limits of the Mahabad Republic, only 16,000 were residents of the city of Mahabad.[24] The main components of the Kurdish state were the huge Shikak and Herki tribes (the latter, one of the last nomadic tribes of the Anatolian plateau), and many other smaller tribes were associated with it. It probably could be argued that the Mahabad Republic was, in fact, never more than the city of Mahabad and that the tribes of the surrounding region paid deference to it out of fear of the Russians. Thus it could be said that Mahabad was protected by the Russians against the tribes.

Eventually, the Russians did sponsor and protect the diminutive republic, but how were they maneuvered into doing so? One always has to move carefully when considering conspiracy theories, but the reader will have noticed that conspiracies are never too far in the background of a great deal of the political activity having to do with the Kurds. In the present case, it seems highly likely that the Russians instigated the autonomy plan, at least for Azerbaijan, in order to manipulate the central government of Iran—that is to say, the Russians would foster a genuine separation of the Azerbaijanis unless the central government granted the USSR an oil concession.[25] The Russians had made a strong bid for such a concession in 1944 but had been rejected by the Iranian government.[26] Balked initially, the Russians then seem to have proceeded on two fronts. Overall, they built up the effectiveness of the communist Tudeh party, which was the only well-organized political party in Iran throughout World War II. They also began encouraging the nationalist and separatist aspirations of the Azerbaijanis.

Azerbaijan has always been a problem for the Persians. Its people compose the largest minority in Iran, and it is the richest province. The Azerbaijanis are Turkomans with ties to the Turks to the west, and a large contingent of them constitute the Soviet Socialist Republic of Azerbaijan. In the 1906 revolution in Iran, the Azerbaijanis provided the crucial element in the anti-Qajar coalition that ensured the revolution's success.

The Azerbaijan Republic formed in 1945 was truly revolutionary. The element that seized power opposed the feudalists—who were effectively alienated— and redistributed the land, nationalized banks, enacted other socialist measures,[27] and opposed the clergy (the Azerbaijanis are Shia Muslims). Thus the revolt in Azerbaijan was one that the Russians could totally approve of, and it brought a thorough system change as well. Had the USSR been primarily interested in the acquisition of territory, it might have supported the Azerbaijan Republic more enthusiastically, but the Russians' subsequent behavior toward it (and toward Mahabad) leads to the conclusion that the USSR was not primarily interested in moving its border south but mainly wanted oil.

After their failure to exact a concession in 1944, the Russians began in earnest to cultivate "progressive" elements among both the Azerbaijanis and the Kurds. In Kurdistan the organization the Russians favored was a club formed in 1943 called the Komala (Komala i zhian i Kurdistan [Committee for the Resurrection of Kurdistan]), which was the focus of intellectual and political dissension. With a membership made up mostly of young people, who in the main devoted themselves to composing literary works extolling the ideal of Kurdish nationhood,[28] this group was similar to the literary-cum-nationalist societies of Lebanon and Egypt around 1875 in that it was as much a cultural as a political organization.

Originally, the Komala's membership was restricted to a small group (fifteen is probably not an underestimate) of city-bred Kurds,[29] but in 1944, it began to expand its activities by enrolling several tribal chiefs. One would have expected the chiefs to suspect such an organization or to treat it as of no account, so their joining seems to indicate a desire to curry favor with the Russians.[30] In September 1945, the Komala was invited to use the Soviet Union's cultural center in Mahabad as club headquarters. At this point, the Komala, soon to be transformed into the Kurdish Democratic party (in November 1945), was quite free of tribal influence. Moreover, it included among its members people of all classes.[31]

However, the man who was to dominate the Mahabad Republic was a representative of the old aristocracy of Mahabad, Qazi Mohammad. Qazi was a religious figure, and his was one of the leading families of Mahabad.[32] He was an authoritarian and for this reason remained—or rather, was kept—outside the circle of the Komala for a year after it was formed.[33] When he finally was invited to join in October 1944, he justified the misgivings of the original members by taking over. One version, perhaps apocryphal, indicates that Qazi was useful to the Russians: The Komala, made up mostly of young men, tended to be inconveniently democratic; Qazi, on the other hand, could command discipline and serve as an excellent conduit for direction stemming from the USSR's military command.[34]

In September 1945, the Russians invited a group of prominent Kurds to a parley in Tabriz. From there, they were taken by train to Baku,[35] where the prime minister of the Soviet Socialist Republic of Azerbaijan, Baghirov, awaited them. The Russians were bound by their 1942 treaty with the Iranian government to refrain from supporting sedition in those areas under their military control, and perhaps that was the reason why they were most circumspect in their first meeting with the leading Kurds. Baghirov seems to have implied a great deal but to have made no explicit promises. Qazi and the other Kurds came away from the meeting, which lasted two days, with the not quite definite conviction that the Russians would support autonomy for Kurdistan in Mahabad and that the Mahabad Kurds were out of step with the times if they did not act to associate themselves with the democratic movement of peoples worldwide against fascism.[36] The only explicit proposal that seems to have been made was conditional: If the Kurds changed the name of the Komala to the Kurdish Democratic party (KDP), the Russians might see their way clear to funneling funds to it.[37]

Two months after the Russian-initiated meeting in Baku, Tudeh elements in Azerbaijan seized control of the provincial government in Tabriz and took over the province. The Kurds were still politically naive, as previously stated, but they were not lambs. It must have appeared plain to them which way the wind was blowing and that they ought to take a correct stand, *now.*

Two events occurred shortly after the Baku meeting that seem to have confirmed the Mahabad Kurds in their conviction to commit themselves irredeemably: the appearance of the

Barzanis and the arrival of Russian arms. At the end of September 1945, the Barzanis appeared in Iran asking for asylum from the pursuing Iraqi army, and the Mahabad Kurds invited them in. The Iranian Kurdish tribes that had joined the republic had done so out of fear of the Soviet Union, and surviving tribes in Iran were demoralized, like the majority of those in Iraq. Having been forced to come to terms with the Iranian central government, the Kurdish tribes could not be relied upon to fight against it unless it appeared to be in their interests to do so. The townsmen-leaders of the Mahabad Republic would hardly appear to be fit warrior-partners for the feudal chiefs, but the Barzanis were another matter for they were fighters of true mettle. The Mahabad Republic had received an extremely valuable gift, nothing less than the services of one of the last of the "unspoiled" fighting tribes that followed the tradition of the Wolves of Kurdistan. However, there was a potential problem. Would the primitive Barzanis be able to work with the Mahabad leaders, who were sponsored by the Soviet Union?

In December, the Russians backed up their promise of assistance. The Kurds had expected money, but none was forthcoming; instead, trucks arrived with 1,200 rifles and ample ammunition.[38] It must be kept in mind that the Kurds had been disarmed by Reza Shah and forbidden to wear their national costume. Now, all at once, all the bonds were coming off, and the turbans, baggy pantaloons, and gorgeous stomachers blossomed again in the streets of Mahabad. The transformation taking place in the winter of 1945–1946 was enormous. In the circumstances it is not at all surprising that the leading Kurds of Mahabad lost all restraint and recklessly committed themselves and the people of that city to a revolutionary course.

On January 22, 1946, the KDP called a convocation of the entire city of Mahabad. Qazi appeared dressed in a Russian general's uniform (much was to be made of this fact at his subsequent trial), retaining his white turban to signify his religious status,[39] and proclaimed the creation of the Mahabad

Republic. Photographs of the event testify that the affair was well attended: The square in which the proclamation was made (Chawr Chira) was crowded, and people lined the rooftops surrounding it.[40] A Russian, Major Yermakov, was present (a point that was to become significant later when the Russians reproached the Kurds for having acted without consultation in proclaiming the republic).

What did the Russians want from the Kurds and what did the Kurds think they were getting away with? If we assume that the Russians' main aim was to pressure the Iranian government into granting the USSR an oil concession, then setting up two republics in the northwestern corner of Iran made no sense. In fact, Mahabad was bound to give trouble. Kurds are Kurds, and Azerbaijanis are Azerbaijanis. Because of districting, some Kurds happened to land in a province that was predominantly Azerbaijani, and that province had been marked by the Russians for use as a bargaining chip in discussions about the oil concession. But once an independent Kurdish entity was established (as one now irrevocably had been), other Kurds would seek to join it—particularly the mass of Kurds dwelling elsewhere in Iran—but incorporating these Kurds into the Mahabad Republic would only cause trouble because the bulk of Iranian Kurdistan was in the British sphere.

All in all it can be argued that the Kurds had done precisely what the Russians did not want them to do. In their original interview with Baghirov he had explicitly suggested that Mahabad be incorporated into the autonomous Azerbaijan Republic, and Qazi is supposed to have made it equally explicit that the Kurds had in mind the formation of a Greater Kurdistan.

The Makeup of the Mahabad Republic

William Eagleton gives a useful breakdown of the cabinet of the new republic by status. After the president, Qazi, came the prime minister, a religious figure; the war minister, Qazi's cousin; the minister of education, a member of the upper class; the minister of the interior, a garage mechanic; the minister of health, a member of the upper class; the ministers of foreign affairs and roads, both members of the upper class; the ministers of economics and labor, both from second-rank families; the minister of posts, from a good family; the minister of commerce, from the upper class; the minister of justice, a religious figure; and the minister of agriculture, a youth trained in an agricultural high school.[41] All these cabinet ministers were city-bred Kurds, and all were a part of a vanguard of Kurdish intellectualism. To be sure, there were more-profound intellects in the traditional centers of Kurdish dynamism, as-Sulaymaniyah and Damascus, but the Mahabadis were sympathetic to the progressive currents of nationalism as it was practiced in the more cosmopolitan areas of the world. They may not have understood the theoretical importance of a proper political organization, but in the KDP they had copied the cell system applied by the Communists, who were past masters at structuring subversive political movements.

Very little rhetoric, at least of the Marxist type, was produced by the KDP, but there was a great deal of obsessive pamphleteering of all sorts, which was significant. Recall that in Turkey, Kurdishness was literally outlawed; in Iran, prior to the Mahabad Republic, the Kurds were so oppressed as to be all but eradicated as a separate people; in Iraq, the decomposition of the tribal system was being brought about by commercialization. Now, in Iran, there was an unexpected efflorescence of Kurdish letters, and these tracts circulated widely throughout the Kurdish areas of the Middle East. But perhaps most noteworthy, when focusing on the ideological accomplishments of the tiny, short-lived state, are the excesses that it avoided.

To the north, in Tabriz, the Azerbaijanis could not escape the side effects of real revolutionary change. Driving the feudalists off the land won the revolutionary government implacable enemies, which necessitated the creation of a secret police apparatus, with informers and all of the wretched paraphernalia of state terror.[42] By contrast, the Kurdish Mahabad Republic was remarkably free of intimidation of any sort.[43] The Kurds tuned into broadcasts wherever they could be received, and there was a constant interchange of information between Tehran and Mahabad. A Soviet-supplied printing press turned out reams of Kurdish nationalist material, and elementary-school books were printed in Kurdish. Of course, one reason—perhaps the only significant reason—the republic was so free is that it did not produce a great deal of social legislation.

Finances were not a problem for the new republic as the region has always produced a high-grade tobacco. One year, when Tehran understandably refused to buy the year's consignment, which it had contracted to do, the Russians bought it for $800,000, which was less than what Tehran had agreed to pay, but the net return was greater because the Russian transaction involved no payoffs to middlemen.[44] At one point, the Kurds borrowed $4,400 from the Azerbaijanis and repaid the loan with sugar produced at a factory in Mindowab northeast of Mahabad.[45] There was smuggling, an age-old source of revenue in the Zagros Mountains, and taxes were collected as they had been under the authority of Tehran. Indeed, no change was wrought in the collecting of taxes at all. As the republic drifted further and further out of the orbit of Tehran, more and more Iranian nationals working as tax collectors in Mahabad left, and their posts were taken by Kurds[46] who went on collecting in the same old way, but now the money stayed in Mahabad. There were also levies on wealthy families of the region who were lukewarm in their support of the new republic.[47] Unfortunately, we have no record of the system of tax collecting, and we do not know how individual assessments were apportioned. We must assume, however, that because the landowning, commercial class was never alienated from the republic, the exactments on that class could not have been great.

Qazi Mohammad received no salary as president—indeed he refused one.[48] Other cabinet members took sixty-five dollars a month.[49] Whenever the tribes were billeted outside of Mahabad in defense of the republic, an officer of the Mahabad army was assigned to provide food. Thus the evil tendency of Kurdish tribesmen to loot was overcome—a tendency that ordinarily, in the absence of any other means of provisioning, was inevitable.[50]

The services provided by the republic are obvious from the list of cabinet positions given above. In addition, instruction in Kurdish was instituted in the schools, several Kurdish periodicals were published regularly, and a Kurdish theater was formed.[51] The republic was also attentive to petitions addressed to it. A twelve-man supreme council was formed, and its members were mainly from the aristocratic families.[52] This group was constituted solely to receive petitions from the citizens.

But perhaps the most significant innovation of all related to the army. The leaders of Mahabad were apparently aware of the fatal complication that had undercut all previous Kurdish nationalist schemes. The city Kurds, who had generally mounted such efforts, had been basically dependent for protection on the *agha*s and their fighting tribesmen, the most backward element in Kurdish society. So in Mahabad an army was formed. The effort was modest—at peak strength the army had only 70 officers, 40 noncommissioned officers, and 1,200 privates[53]—but these members were nontribal Kurds who had been mobilized. With the ratio of nontribal to tribal Kurds increasing at a rapid rate, a start toward mobilizing these previously disaffected people was long overdue. The Soviet Union supplied instructors,[54] and the recruits were taught how to drive trucks, drill, shoot, and use grenades.[55] Deserters from the Iraqi army also served as officers in this first attempt to introduce military discipline to the Kurds.

The mainstay of the republic throughout its existence, was the Barzanis. Many writers laud their uniqueness as "a tribe which could fight away from its home-territory"[56] and which would keep to the field without looting. An examination of the history of the Kurds shows us that this behavior was not so extraordinary. The Hamawand had penetrated several hundred miles into the Russian Caucasus in 1877 in a cohesive raiding party and had returned in a body.[57] To be sure, the lure was loot, but when the same tribe—or a section of it— was relocated to Tripoli in North Africa, it maintained tribal discipline while it fought its way home to Iraq. The behavior of the Barzanis appears extraordinary only because true tribal organization had all but died out everywhere else.

The Barzanis served the republic out of the direst necessity. Having fled their home area, they had nowhere else to go. Other Iraqi tribes had become demoralized and had decomposed, but the Barzanis, in the remoteness of their home territory, had been protected from commercialization effected by the British. The tribe's chiefs, Mulla Mustafa and Shaikh Ahmad, were not plutocrats—their homes differed from those of their followers only in that they were of stone. Architecturally, the design of their homes was Spartan, their diet was Spartan also,[58] and they dressed in rough homespun. But most important from the point of view of tribal organization, the Barzani tribesmen were freeholders, not tenants. Moreover, they had never been regularly subsidized. In 1919, when the British were doling out subsidies, the Barzanis had alienated themselves from consideration by murdering two British political officers,[59] so the Barzanis, unlike so many tribes to the south, never grew fat on British bounty.

The Last Days of Mahabad

The Russians had delivered 1,200 weapons to the Kurds in December 1945, and they produced a further consignment of 5,000 rifles in February 1946. The republic wanted tanks and planes and artillery,[60] but it never got those (understandably, since from the Russian point of view, such supplies would have been too destabilizing for the whole region to be considered). In April 1946, the Barzanis, armed with the pick of the Russian rifles, moved to close off the Saqqez–Sar Dasht road in order to isolate the Iranian garrison at Sar Dasht.

The leaders of the republic had intended to strike for Sanandaj, but they were dissuaded by the Russians, who argued that the British would not accept such a provocation. Still, as affairs developed, the Iranians were to force the Barzanis' hand.

On April 24, a small Iranian force probing north of Saqqez fell into a Barzani ambush, and twenty-one Iranian soldiers were killed; seventeen wounded; and forty taken prisoner. The Iranian military then negotiated an arrangement with the Barzanis whereby supplies could reach the beleaguered garrison.[61] Being able to exact minor, but nonetheless real, concessions from the state of Iran buoyed the confidence of the leaders of the republic.

However, this confidence produced unfortunate complications when the two main tribal supports of the Mahabad Republic, the Herki and Shikak, began harassing the Azerbaijani towns of Shahpur, Khoi, and Rezaiyeh. The Herki and the Shikak so pressed their assault that the Russians were drawn in to arrange a peace. Ultimately, the republics of Azerbaijan and Mahabad drew up a seven-point treaty of mutual understanding, and two of the articles were remarkable.

Article 3. The two Governments will form a Joint Economic Committee to deal with economic problems, and the decisions of the Committee will be observed by the heads of both states.

Article 6. The Government of Azerbaijan will take steps to contribute to the cultural and linguistic progress of the Kurds living in its territory, and vice versa.[62]

This agreement sincerely shocked the Iranian authorities since both articles clearly flouted Tehran's sovereignty by referring to two separate states. If the Tehran government had not wanted to admit so previously, it was now undeniable that a part of its territory was in the process of breaking away.

The Mahabad-Azerbaijan agreement was struck in April 1946. In the same month, the Soviet Union was informed by Prime Minister Qavam es-Satlaneh of Iran that he was amenable to an oil concession (51 percent Russian, 49 percent Iranian); however, the concession must be approved by the Majlis, which would take no action until all the foreign troops had quit Iran. The Russians suggested to the Azerbaijanis, their main clients, that they come to terms with Tehran, and Jafar Pishovari, the president of the Azerbaijan Republic, accordingly traveled to Tehran on April 29 to commence negotiations. The Azerbaijanis wanted autonomy within the framework of the Iranian state, which Tehran was in a mood to concede. However, they also wanted a private army; Azerbaijani recruits would not serve in the army of Iran.[63] The Iranian military balked at this stipulation, and no agreement was reached. Pishovari returned to Tabriz, where the Russians, now apparently determined to evacuate Iran so the concession could be voted, insisted he concede.

In the meantime, Qazi, too, traveled to Tehran with a proposal for putting Kurdish autonomy on a legal basis. Qavam proposed that Mahabad abstract itself from the province of Azerbaijan and be reconstituted into an enlarged province of Kurdistan, which would become autonomous. Qazi agreed to this on the condition that the Russians agree also.[64] Perhaps as foreseen by Qavam, the Russians rejected the proposal.

When the Russian troops quit Iran in May 1946, the Azerbaijanis dropped their demand for exclusive control over Azerbaijani arms, and an arrangement for the autonomy of their republic was worked out. The Russians then expected that the oil concession would be voted on, but at this point, the Iranians introduced new conditions. They insisted that not only must all foreign troops be evacuated but that all areas of the country must be reoccupied by the Iranian army.[65] The Russians overcame Azerbaijani resistance by assuring their clients that only a token Iranian force would enter the region. The Russians' behavior throughout seems to have been cynically exploitative—at least of the Azerbaijanis. If we accept the fact that the Russians never intended that there should be two breakaway republics, then we must conclude that the Kurds rashly compromised themselves.

Once the Russian army was out of the country and the Iranian army had returned to the northwest, the fate of the two republics was sealed. The whole episode in fact ended in a debacle for all parties, but the calamitous ending of the republics was deferred for a time. The Iranians had to go slowly, because the Russians might reenter the country. First, the shah ordered Qavam to stand down, and his government, in which there were three Tudeh party members, fell. The new government, free of Tudeh representation, presented the proposal for a Russian concession—and the Majlis rejected it. At that point, the Russians might have exercised their option of reoccupying northwestern Iran, but coincidentally, the British raised the tribes in the south, the Bakhtiaris and the Qashqai.[66] The old game was being replayed: Any move by the Russians in the north would invite a corresponding British move in the south. The Russians did not move but the Iranian army did—straight on Tabriz. The Azerbaijan Republic collapsed ignominiously on December 13, 1946; Mahabad surrendered the next day.

It is instructive to contrast the passing of the two republics. The collapse of Azerbaijan unleashed an orgy of recrimination, and some officials of the republic were torn apart by the mobs.[67] In Mahabad the end of the republic was greeted with resignation but no recrimination.[68] Barzani, in fact, tried to get Qazi and the rest of the government to flee, but in the end, they did not and were on hand to deliver the city to the Iranian army. The tribes turned on the republic, but even then there was no violence. Largely because the Iranian military kept the tribes in the dark, they were caught unawares when the troops marched in.

Qazi, his brother Abdul Qasim, and his cousin Saif i Qazi, were tried and hanged. The main facts against them were that Mahabad had its own flag and officials had permitted themselves to be photographed in Russian uniforms. A map of Greater Kurdistan was produced at the trial,[69] but probably most damning was a letter from Qazi to the Iranian commander at Saqqez, which read, in part, "You are the officers of an army which, at the time of fighting and risking lives, takes to your heels and traduce Firdausi's great lines of poetry: 'We turn our backs to the enemy one by one, rather than die for our country.'"[70]

With the fall of the Mahabad Republic, the fate of the Barzanis was in doubt. Mulla Mastafa succeeded in holding the Iranian army at bay so successfully that a stalemate developed. To break it, the Iranian commander, Razmara, agreed to allow Mulla Mustafa to travel to Tehran where he attempted to induce the British to guarantee amnesty for his tribe to return to Iraq.[71] The British refused. The Iranian government suggested instead that the Barzanis permit themselves to be disarmed and settled at Hamawand near the Iran-Iraq border. After first seeming to agree, Barzani rejected the proposal.

In April 1947, the main body of the tribe, under Shaikh Ahmad, recrossed into Iraq. The shaikh was imprisoned, and four army officers who had deserted the Iraqi army were hanged.[72] Mulla Mustafa and between 500 and 800 picked tribesmen then began trekking north, zigzagging back and forth across the borders of Iraq, Iran, and Turkey in a march that lasted fourteen days, during which time they successfully avoided the armies of all three states (except for one clash in which the Iranians were worsted). On June 10, the Barzanis crossed the Aras River into Russia where they were to remain for eleven years.

6
The Nationalist Movement in Crisis

We take up the discussion of the Kurdish question again in 1958, for little of importance happened in the interval from 1947 to 1958. By the latter year, the situation in the Middle East was very different from that of the years immediately preceding. All sorts of new forces had been let loose, not the least of which was Nasserism (or Pan-Arabism, for there was not much difference). In 1958, Gamel Abdel Nasser seemed to be on the point of controlling a significant portion of the Middle East's oil supply.[1] In that year, he agreed to form a union with Syria (the United Arab Republic), which gave him access to the oil pipeline across Syria; and in July, it appeared he had control of the oil at the wellhead also when pro-Nasser elements (or so they were believed to be) in the Iraqi army seized power. There was nothing now to stop Iraq from being pulled into the union, and Nasser's stock could not have been higher.

In the United States it was generally believed that Nasser was a Communist,[2] because of his acceptance of Soviet arms and his negotiations with the Russians to build the Aswan Dam. In England, Nasser was compared to Hitler,[3] apparently not on the basis of any precise similarity but because of intense hatred. Nasser had nationalized the Suez Canal (partly British owned) and had survived the 1956 war, in which Britain had been humiliated. The sudden accession of Iraq into the orbit of Arab nationalism seemed an excess of good fortune for the Egyptian leader—unfortunately for him, however, the arrangement with Iraq did not work out.

Nasser was foiled in Iraq by a combination of factors: Iraqi particularism, which, though latent, was strong; Communist opposition; and, finally, an unwillingness on the part of the Kurds to facilitate Pan-Arab arrangements in Iraq. In this chapter we will look at the further association of the Kurdish nationalist movement with the forces of Communism in the Middle East. Many writers specifically downplay this association or, like Dana Adams Schmidt, condone it as a "marriage of necessity."[4] We will see that Communist-Kurdish cooperation was natural and that the association of the Iraqi Kurds with the Iraqi Communist party was of long standing.

The combination of Communists and Kurds was based on like interests. After the 1958 revolution in Iraq, the Communists called for federation with Egypt, opposing the Arab nationalists' scheme for union,[5] in an attempt at a compromise to keep Iraq free of Arab nationalism, which to the Communists would be a backward step. The Communists believed that they would be submerged if Iraq joined the Syrian-Egyptian union, and the Kurds viewed the alliance in much the same light. Arab nationalists looked to the expansion of Iraq's frontiers as that country merged into a grander entity; the Kurdish nationalists wished to see those frontiers drawn inward, with Iraq halved into a cantonal arrangement: Arab Iraq and Kurdish Iraq. For very different reasons therefore, the Kurds and the Communists saw eye to eye on the question of the union.

The long-standing relationship between the Communists and the Kurds arose because of the fundamental incompatibility of the Kurdish nationalists with the liberal parties of the Arab Left, all of which, without exception, were Arab nationalist. Kurds, therefore, naturally gravitated toward the Communists. Indeed, Batatu claims that in Iraqi Communist history the period 1949–1955 "may not inappropriately be identified as the period of the ascendancy of the Kurds. . . . The Kurds not only provided all the general secretaries but accounted for as high as 31.3% of the entire membership of the Central Committee."[6] Batatu theorizes that it was the relative inaccessibility of Kurdistan that preserved the Communists there and that the Communists went out of their way to cultivate intellectual Kurds, realizing that they could not agree with the Arab parties. Also, Iraqi Kurds had followed the exploits of the Barzanis at Mahabad, and it could not have hurt the Communists in the Kurds' eyes that the Kurdish national hero had chosen exile in the Soviet Union.

Once again, Kurdish nationalist development focused on Iraq where there was an extraordinary efflorescence of Kurdish self-assertion, for the most part under leftist auspices. However, before recounting the Kurdish-Iraqi-Arab struggle, we should examine the way in which the international situation at the time affected Iraqi politics generally and Kurdish political consciousness in particular.

The International Situation

The significant international event involving Iraq in the Middle East prior to 1958 was the Baghdad Pact, signed in 1955. The mandate system, which had been put into effect after World War I, had really been a device to preserve the gains of empires that were too weak to maintain themselves by sheer power.[7] Had Britain and France been individually strong, neither would have needed the collective security guarantees that were provided by the mandate system. Now, after World War II, and particularly after the creation of Israel, Britain needed those guarantees once more if it was to hold on in the Middle East, and the Baghdad Pact was put together as a way of finessing the United States into a more or less subordinate role.

Iraq, Britain's client (whereas Turkey, also a candidate to head a Western-oriented defense arrangement, was the client of the United States), was to become the linchpin of a new regional defense arrangement. The alliance was to be southward looking toward Arab lands, where Britain—its expertise based on long-standing associations—would play a leading role. The drawback of the Baghdad Pact was that it ignored over 100 years of Arab political development. The Arabs had been relentlessly trying to squeeze the imperialists out of the region, particularly Britain and France, and had reduced imperial control to a few isolated holdings—in particular, air bases such as Habbaniya in Iraq. Now, Britain was preparing, in effect, to revivify its Middle East presence through a pact that the Arabs believed was spurious. All Arab nationalists condemned the pact—even Hashemite Jordan was cowed into silence. Yet Hashemite Iraq, under strongman Nuri as-Said, was supposed to serve as the Pact's foundation stone.

Had the pact provided benefits for the Iraqis, it might ultimately have proved a good thing, but it did not provide for any evident improvement in Iraq's situation. All Iraq got was the cooperation of Turkey, Iran, Pakistan, and Great Britain against Communism. In all other areas Iraq was shortchanged, even in the military one, where payoffs could have been expected with respect to guns and training and heightened prestige for the Iraqi military. But Nuri and the Hashemites distrusted the military (for good reason, as we shall see), and kept it on a short string. The economic condition of Iraq did not sufficiently improve as a result of the pact. Foreign specialists advised that oil and agriculture be developed,[8] but the country's oil industry was in the hands of the Americans and Europeans; its agriculture, in those of the owners of great landed estates. By pouring cash into land reclamation schemes, irrigation, and transportation, Nuri hoped to build up the economic base of Iraq gradually—the "trickledown approach," under which it would have taken forever for the dwellers in the mud huts to perceive any change.

Left alone, Nuri and the oligarchs who depended on him might have preserved themselves, but the pact became an issue. Nasser's propaganda was, as always, vicious. Manipulating transistor technology, which had just begun to sweep the Middle East, he villified Nuri and the Hashemites as lackeys and lickspittles, hirelings of the imperialists; the Baghdad Pact served the interests of the imperialists and betrayed the great Arab nation. (Interestingly, despite this line of attack, the pact proved an anathema to the Kurds as well. Ibrahim Ahmad, secretary-general of the Kurdish Democratic party, called it "that holy alliance against the Kurds.")[9] The pact, in combination with Iraq's overall depressed economic condition, would have been too much of a liability even for a regime that was popular—and the Hashemites were never that. When the end came, with Colonel Abdul Karim Kassem's coup in July 1958, the reaction of the Iraqi mob was awful: Nuri's murdered corpse was mutilated, and the royal family was machine-gunned in the palace courtyard.

That the July revolution was motivated to a significant degree by class resentment is shown by the army officers' zeal to enact land reform—something that had been proposed only once, vaguely, under the Hashemites and dropped. One of the first acts of the Kassem regime after the coup was to promulgate a land reform program after the example of Nasser's. However, the revolutionaries in Iraq showed more solicitude for the welfare of the giant landholders than the Egyptians had. In Egypt no one was permitted to hold more than 250 *dunum*s of land; In Iraq the permissible holding was 1,000 *dunum*s for irrigated land and 2,000 *dunum*s for rainwatered land. However, even these limitations could be manipulated as an original owner was allowed to deed property to close relatives.[10]

The Communists exploited this issue of landholding in the internal struggle for power. As their influence increased, they made common cause with the Kurds who scrambled up along with them, emerging as their partners after a revolt in Mosul.

The Communist-Kurdish Partnership

On March 8, 1959, Abdul Wahab Shawaf, commander of the local garrison in Mosul, proclaimed a revolt, the professed aim of which was to topple Kassem and effect union with Egypt. This revolt was brutally crushed by the Communists, who were organized as the People's Revolutionary Force (a

Kassem creation, used by the Communists as a power base), and the Kurds, who were ordered into Mosul by Mulla Mustafa Barzani. The revolt was a political ploy, and it triggered a hellish reaction. To understand these two facts we must examine Mosul's social situation.

Mosul in 1958–1959 was a unique city in Iraq. It was the scene of deep-seated antagonisms, some dating back to the peace settlement of World War I. Up to that time, the city had been a hub of trade, and its commercial connections had stretched west to Syria and north to Turkey.[11] When the peace settlement allotted Mosul to Iraq, trade languished, and in time, prominent Mosuli citizens resigned themselves to furthering their careers in Baghdad. In addition, the social structure of the city was extremely rigid, with Turkomans and wealthy Kurds who had become Turkified under the Ottomans living apart from other Kurds and Assyrians in the poorer quarters.[12]

When the revolt broke out on March 8, all the resentments boiled over: The rich, landed families and their clients, who were pitted against Kassem and land reform, were joined by middle-class officers who distrusted the Communist influence in government; opposed to them were the Communists and the lower-class Kurds—supported by Barzani's tribesmen. The anti-Kassem elements were quickly overwhelmed, and the ensuing suppression was outrageous: There were jeep-draggings, live burials, drumhead trials staged in the city squares, and summary executions after "sentencing."[13] After the Mosul revolt, Communist power was manifest. The party could now look to consolidate itself by advancing specific demands, most notably for direct participation in the cabinet. Kassem, however, displayed extraordinary agility in order to survive as a relatively free agent. Immediately after the Mosul affair, he appeared to give in to the Communists. He reshuffled his cabinet and appointed four new ministers—two of them were identified as party members, and another was pronouncedly leftist.[14] At the same time, however, Kassem was preparing to confront the Communists later on, and this confrontation came at

Kirkuk in July 1959. The Communists had an opportunity to repeat the "success" of Mosul, but Kassem turned the tables on them instead. Accounts vary as to whether the Kirkuk eruption was indeed of Communist manufacture,[15] or a Kurdish-inspired race riot. Many Kurds held high posts in the Communist party, and the case has been made that the Kirkuk massacre actually was an ethnic event—Kurds against their long-standing rivals, the Turkomans. Kirkuk was the site of Iraq's major oil installation, and as such, it acted as a magnet for cheap labor, which was mainly Kurdish. As in Mosul, the ethnic and class divisions in the city were sharp. One-third of the population was Kurdish and one-half Turkoman, the rest being Assyrian Christians (allied with the Kurds along class lines). The Turkomans were wealthy and, along with wealthier Kurds, composed the city's elite. The incident that provoked the massacre seems trivial: a question of precedence in a procession commemorating the revolution. Kurdish marching units and Turkomans quarreled, blows were exchanged, then shots—finally the Kurds overwhelmed the Turkomans. Kassem, viewing the photographs of the massacre victims, is supposed to have remarked, "Hugulu never perpetrated anything like this." The Kurds had been marching as representatives of Communist organizations, and it was easy, therefore, to manipulate the incident against the Communists. In fact, Kassem took the opportunity to distance himself from them. Castigating the forces of anarchy that would destroy the country, he gave the Iraqi foes of the Communists cause to hope that their position might be strengthened.

The Communists' fortunes had peaked as of July 1959, whether they knew it or not, and never again would they climb so high. Kassem did not cut the Communists off entirely but tied them up in a complex of bureaucratic hamstringing, involving the Association Laws, which effectively denied them official party status. Until this time, the Kurds had been strong allies of the Communists and were clearly affected by the latter's fall from power. The Kurds were somewhat isolated—

in which awkward position their leader, Barzani, would now further isolate them.

The Return of Mulla Mustafa Barzani

Not a great deal is known about Barzani's activities from 1947 to 1958 while he was in the Soviet Union. There are reports that he studied at a Russian military college, that he learned Russian,[16] and that he spent his early years there in Baku assisting with the preparation of propaganda broadcasts beamed to Kurdistan. Schmidt says that for the first part of his enforced exile, Barzani was held in limbo because the USSR's security chief, Lavrenti Beria, mistrusted him—his suspicions aroused by his lieutenant, a Turkoman and therefore someone who traditionally mistrusted Kurds[17]—and that Barzani's treatment at the hands of the Russians is supposed to have improved after Beria's execution in 1953. The Russians enrolled the Barzani tribesmen in schools of carpentry and mechanics and the more-educated ones in interpreters' schools and schools of medicine.[18] Some Barzanis married Russian women, whom they subsequently brought back to Iraq.

Barzani received word of Kassem's successful coup while traveling in Czechoslovakia[19] and cabled home immediately. Kassem agreed to grant Barzani and his followers amnesty, and they returned to Iraq. Barzani flew home, arriving in Baghdad in October 1958, and some 850 of his followers arrived in Basrah by Russian ship in April 1959. Barzani flew by way of Cairo where he met with Nasser, but their discussions were never made public.

On his return to Baghdad, the Kurdish guerilla leader received a hero's welcome from the Kurds who crowded the airport, wearing their traditional dress, singing folk songs, and performing their traditional dances. Kassem greeted Barzani with a great show of friendship, which Barzani, in subsequent interviews, claims to have suspected.[20] Kassem had definite ideas about the role Barzani was to play under the auspices of the new regime. He put Barzani on a monthly subsidy and gave him a luxury villa—also a limousine (perhaps that of the late Nuri as-Said).[21] Barzani was not, however, permitted to return to Barzan.

In their first serious exchange Kassem insisted that Barzani assume the presidency of the Kurdish Democratic party of Iraq (KDP, not to be confused with the KDP of Mahabad, with which its ties were slight).[22] On Barzani's return, Ibrahim Ahmad, the secretary-general of the party, had made him an offer of the presidency, which Barzani initially refused but later accepted.[23] Throughout his career he scorned the party and Ahmad, whom he found "arrogant" (an opinion that Ahmad returned).[24]

Kassem hoped to control the Kurdish community through Barzani and, by maneuvering to have him made president of the KDP, hoped to institutionalize that control. Kassem viewed the Barzanis as a floating resource. For example, he enrolled the Kurdish fighters in the People's Revolutionary Force (PRF) and returned them (without their leader) to the north, where they took over police and customs operations. They became the watchdogs of Kassem's policy imposed upon the *agha*s, which generated immediate friction. First of all, they had to be provided with land. To do so meant repossessing their former lands, which had been sequestered when they fled to Iran and given to their enemies, and this land reapportionment immediately set the Kurds one against another. Further, the maladministration of the Barzanis got so bad (at one point, it approached semiplundering), the local *agha*s appealed to Kassem to remove all the PRF Barzanis from their territory and to replace them with Arabs.[25] Kassem eventually did so, but not before the Kurdish Lolani tribe rebelled and was bombed into exile by the air force. Other tribes went into voluntary exile in Iran and Turkey rather than submit to the Barzanis (an impressive list is found in Arfa's book).[26]

All this flexing of muscles by Barzani's people went on with their leader in Baghdad. Shut off from the north, Barzani was attempting to control his area in absentia. He went further and put out a call for an international conference of Kurds to be held in Baghdad, but there was little response outside Iraq. The bare notion of such a convocation was potentially so destabilizing for the region that it is surprising that Barzani entertained any hope of its success. He next left Iraq to participate in celebrations of the October revolution in Russia. Uriel Dann claims that Barzani went there to importune the Russians to force Kassem to make concessions to Kurdish nationalists, and that Kassem let him go, knowing he would return empty-handed.[27]

In January 1961, Barzani's field of activities was severely limited. He could not really rule in the north, and he had no say in Kurdish affairs outside Iraq. Only now did he approach the KDP, and he and the party leadership drafted a manifesto in 1961 demanding autonomy for the Kurdish region. Other demands included:

1. that Kurdish become the first official language in the autonomous Kurdish region.
2. that the police and army units stationed in the Kurdish region be entirely Kurdish, and that the words of command be in Kurdish.
3. that the Kurdish provincial government control education, health services, communications, and municipal and rural affairs.
4. that a substantial share of the oil industry revenues of the Mosul-Kirkuk region be spent in Kurdistan.
5. that, although external affairs, defense, and overall financial policy were to be left to the central government, the vice premier, the assistant chief of staff, and the assistant ministers of all ministries should be Kurds.
6. that Kurdish army units be employed outside the Kurdish region only with the consent of the regional authorities, except in the case of an external threat.[28]

This set of demands was extraordinarily arrogant, but Barzani and the rest of the Kurds had cause to be forward at that time. The Iraqi constitution, as redrafted after the revolution, contained reference to the Kurds as "partners" in the Iraqi homeland, and the exact wording confirmed the Kurds' "national (qawmiyya) rights within Iraqi unity (wahda)."[29] This reference is the first of its kind in Iraq's constitutional history.

Kassem responded to the Kurdish manifesto by asserting that the proposals constituted a threat to Iraq's territorial and political integrity.[30] Barzani claimed afterward that he never believed for a minute that Kassem was sincere in his professions of friendship for Kurds and also claimed that Kassem was crazy.[31] This latter opinion of Kassem has subsequently become widely held, but, in fact, Kassem was a much more complex figure, and his downfall was less the result of his mental state than of his situation.

The outstanding fact about Iraq under Kassem was that there was no national unity. Factions abounded, and it was against these factions that Kassem had to constantly protect himself. For the forty-three months that he managed to stay in power, Kassem ruled largely by his wits. Practically all writers attribute his eventual downfall to his inability to institutionalize his leadership—he formed no party, and with the exception of the infamous Mahdawi court, he did not work effectively through any institution. Kassem's was a pathetic one-man operation, and a man in his position needs factions to survive. The more contenders for power, the more Kassem might have hoped to see them cannibalize each other. We may assume that Kassem promoted Barzani as a foil to use against all the factions (the Arab nationalists, the Communists, etc.) that were seeking power when the Kurdish leader returned to Iraq from the Soviet Union.

Mulla Mustafa Barzani's Revolt

In 1945, the Barzani tribe, including allies, numbered some 9,000 people. Its vicissitudes at the hands of the Iranians at Mahabad had weakened it, and when Mulla Mustafa fled to the Soviet Union, Ahmad, the tribe's spiritual leader was jailed in Iraq—he was not released until Kassem granted amnesty in 1958.[32] On the whole, the tribe had suffered, but even during its darkest days, it had amassed credits. Mulla Mustafa's prowess as a guerrilla fighter had been broadcast among the Kurds and transformed into legend, and his trek to the USSR (which lasted fifty-one days, during which time only one of his men was lost) entered the annals of Kurdish history. Among a people whose prestige is built on military prowess, the Barzanis could not have stood higher in 1960, and in addition to Barzani's personal reputation, the tribe had secured a power base in the PRF.

It is significant that when Barzani returned from the Soviet Union, Kassem asked him to make peace with his former enemies—and he refused.[33] Even though kept at a distance from his native hills, the Kurdish chief maneuvered against the Zibaris, Surchis, and Herkis—who had all profited from his tribe's distress. After the Lolanis fled to Turkey because of PRF harassment, the Pishdar tribe fled to Persia. In both cases, the Barzanis appropriated the fugitives' lands, slaughtering the cattle and burning their crops.[34]

The Kassem Regime

As Barzani developed into a genuine power factor north of Baghdad, the old chemistry of Baghdad politics began to operate. Even as Kassem built Barzani up, he prepared countervailing forces to tear him down. Kassem began plotting against Barzani early. In the summer of 1959, Barzani guards intercepted a consignment of arms on its way from Baghdad (evidently from Kassem) to the Zibaris,[35] and in May 1960, Kassem showed favor to the Surchis and Herkis by receiving the chiefs of the two tribes privately during the Fifth Congress of the KDP in Baghdad.[36] This action was a slap at Barzani.

Kassem also moved against Barzani on other fronts: He restricted the operations of the KDP and closed down the party's branches until only two were left. In November 1960, he had Ibrahim Ahmad, publisher of *Khabat*, the Kurds' paper, arrested and charged with sedition;[37] in March 1961, he had

Ahmad charged with the murder of a Khoshnaw notable who was inimical to the KDP. Ahmad protested this extraordinary move, and Kassem backed away, but once released, Ahmad went underground in Baghdad.

There were other, more fundamental provocations. The government appeared to be reneging on its pledge to facilitate the use of Kurdish in the north, and not only had few Kurdish officials been appointed in those districts, but some Kurds had been dismissed. In addition, Kassem wanted to suspend appropriations for the Directorate of General Kurdish Studies and transform it into a mere liaison between the Ministry of Education and the Directorate of Education at as-Sulaymaniyah.[38]

Thus, by the summer of 1961, Kassem had positioned himself to check the Kurdish leader should the latter's land-grabbing acitivities in the north get too far out of hand. He placed certain strong tribes on regular subsidies, and they, pleased with the arrangement, were prepared to challenge Barzani. But all this preparation does not mean that Kassem intended, even at this late date, to eliminate Barzani. Given the devious style of politics Kassem practiced, an argument might be made that he promoted the Zibaris and the other tribes merely to keep Barzani in line.

In March 1961, Barzani took French leave of Kassem and Baghdad and slipped into the hills, leaving behind his son Lokman. No sooner had he gone, than an Arab mob descended on the KDP headquarters, besieging young Lokman and his followers. The Barzanis opened fire, killing several demonstrators, and Lokman was arrested, but the actual break between Barzani and Kassem could still have been avoided. Dann has provided us with an interesting analysis of what was taking place:

> It is certain that neither Kassem nor Mulla Mustafa wished for an outbreak of open warfare. . . . it is equally certain each credited the other with aggressive intentions. Thus Mulla Mustafa and the KDP leadership took it for granted that

> Kassem moved troops to the north in the summer of 1961 for a large-scale attack.... On the other hand, Kassem may be excused for believing that assaults committed ... were made at the order of Mulla Mustafa.[39]

The actual confrontation between Barzani and Kassem was provoked by a third party, a Kurdish chief of the Akou tribe, who resented Kassem's land reform and importuned Barzani to join forces against Kassem. Barzani refused, whereupon the chief of the Akou ambushed a column of Iraqi army troops at Bazyan in northern Iraq, and inflicted scores of casualties.[40] Kassem either in mistaken retaliation or deliberate provocation, bombed Barzan, and this act finally pushed Barzani into action against the government.

The Barzani tribe, allied tribes, and remnants of the Assyrian people (who, having no love for the Iraqi government, threw in their lot with the Barzanis) spread out over the northern hills, seizing gendarmerie posts, closing roads, and eliminating isolated military units. This great rising had the effect of sealing off the north against the government, but it also locked the Barzanis and their allies in—as in a bear pit. Opposing them were all their traditional enemies—those who had not been made to flee to Turkey and Iran (and even they were never permanently put away; they could, and did, return).

After September 1961, when the real violence began among the tribes, Kassem assiduously stayed away from the area. He had supplied the Zibaris and other prime Barzani enemies with arms and cash, and he left it to them to fight it out with Mulla Mustafa, probably because, like Nuri before him, he could not trust his own army. (O'Ballance says that Kassem never allowed the army more than a two-day supply of materiel).[41] In fact, it was not until late September that Kassem even admitted there had been a revolt, and then he blamed the outbreak on the British (who allegedly had supplied £400,000 to instigate it)[42] and the Americans. Devotees of the conspiracy theory might wish to make something of Kassem's difficulties with the British and U.S. oil companies in connection with this charge. (It was in 1961 that the Iraqi government moved to reappropriate 99 percent of the unexploited concession areas held by the oil companies.)

Barzani had an estimated 5,000 fighters, including his allies. Kassem had his Second Division positioned at Kirkuk[43] but did not move it. In addition to having to worry about the ambitions of his fellow officers, Kassem was bedeviled by the problem of the ethnic composition of the Kirkuk force as one-third of the Second Division was Kurdish.[44] However, in the early part of the revolt there was not much desertion (that started in earnest after nationalism began to exert an appeal). Prudently, Kassem had increased the army's pay, once in November 1958 and again in January 1959,[45] so there were strong inducements for the soldiers to stay loyal—though, at the same time, being killed in the Kurdish highlands could not have been an appealing prospect. As long as the Zibaris and the Herkis—the progovernment tribes—were willing to bear the brunt of the fighting, Kassem was not disposed to commit his regular forces.

Kassem did make prodigal use of his small but lethal air force—about six fighter squadrons of Hunter and MiG jets and one squadron of Ilyushin-28 fighter bombers[46]—against the Barzanis, and the air terror set a pattern for a whole series of anticivilian outrages. The Barzani troops could evade the jet fighters since the jets' supererogatory speed made them unsuitable for attacking guerrilla fighters, strung out over a craggy landscape and hiding in the shadows, but the planes could, and did, flatten towns and wreak havoc on the villagers. (Statistics for this war, as with most statistics relating to the Kurds, are unreliable; but one often quoted is that between September and October 1961, 1,270 Kurdish villages were destroyed by air sorties.)[47]

In October, Kassem anticipated that the Kurds would interrupt their operations when winter came and called off the invasion. But the Barzanis did not relax their efforts. They reoccupied their villages, and those of their tribal enemies, and soon they controlled a crescent 300 miles long and 70 miles wide from the Syrian frontier to Khanaqin. Kassem, learning of this development, ordered his troops to take over from the anti-Barzani tribes—a gesture only, for the Iraqi army could not take on the Kurds in the mountains in wintertime. Perhaps in desperation, Kassem began rounding up KDP members who were still in Baghdad.

One of the strongest pieces of evidence that Barzani had not intended to defy the government (but, rather, merely to aggrandize himself at his tribal enemies' expense) is supplied by the behavior of the KDP after the outbreak of the revolt. It did nothing initially and then vacillated for quite a time. In early 1961, one KDP leader, Jelal Telebani, had complained to Barzani about Kassem (who was to dissolve the party in September). When approached for his counsel, Barzani cautioned restraint. Thus, when Barzani pounced on the gendarmerie posts—in a general clearing of the northern region of government units—the KDP was caught off guard.

Ibrahim Ahmad did not want the KDP to join the rising. He argued that the KDP politicians must act upon the lessons of Mahabad, which they had supposedly absorbed.[48] What was taking place in the mountains was purely a tribal affair, and what Barzani was doing was no different from the actions of Shaikh Mahmud in an earlier time: setting himself up as a traditional war leader and expanding his landholdings at the expense of his enemies. Tribalists were notoriously unreliable, Ahmad charged. Further, this time, in contrast to Mahabad, the Kurds enjoyed no international support. (There is no convincing evidence that either the United States or the USSR meddled in this first revolt of Barzani; certainly, neither supplied any heavy arms.) The youthful Telebani argued an opposing viewpoint. He and Omar Mustafa, a member of the KDP Central Committee, attached great significance to the fact that so much of Kassem's army was Kurdish—and therefore presumably unreliable.[49] Nevertheless, the KDP certainly was discomfited by being caught unawares when its president went to war. Why, if Barzani were launching a national war of liberation, as he later claimed, did he not bother to inform the leaders of his own party? The answer would appear to be that Ibrahim Ahmed's assessment was correct. In 1961, Barzani was behaving no differently from Kurdish chiefs of times past: Sensing a power vacuum developing in Iraq, he and his tribe had set out to fill it.

In effect, then, the ideological character of the war was grafted on after the initiation of hostilities between Barzani and Kassem when the KDP finally decided, in December 1961, to throw in its lot with Barzani and even then, Barzani refused to permit the KDP leaders to set up their forces in his war zone.[50] Ultimately, a rough division of territory was worked out whereby the KDP manned the southern front— around Mount Sarband in the north, as-Sulaymaniyah in the south, and Kirkuk in the west—and the Barzani forces operated in the area north of that to the Turkish border. Barzani told Dana Adams Schmidt that the KDP was next to worthless in the military phase of the revolt[51]—neither a charitable nor an accurate view. Schmidt quotes Telebani's claim by way of rebuttal, that the KDP had to work up a fighting force from scratch. When the leadership went north to fight in December, it had only thirty recruits and, says Telebani, no weapons to speak of (Telebani had a bird gun, a gift from Barzani after the latter's visit to the Soviet Union).[52]

Barzani resumed his operations against Kassem in the spring of 1962. Kassem responded in March by offering amnesty to all Kurdish rebels who would lay down their arms, and Barzani replied that he would agree to stop fighting if Kassem would relinquish his leadership and a democratic government was created. Two other events of note occurred in March. Barzani stated publicly that the Kurds were fighting for autonomy, not independence, an announcement that appealed to Arabs in the capital and abroad who were unhappy with the attack on the Kurds (judging correctly that it weakened the state of Iraq in particular and Arabs in general). Also in March, the KDP established bases in four areas and began functioning as full-fledged participants in the struggle.

Throughout the spring and summer of 1962, the Iraqi government's campaign against the Barzanis languished. When the army managed to strike deep into Kurdish territory, the Barzanis, in true guerrilla fashion, would always give ground, but they would rarely give way. Thus, a column would be permitted to penetrate the rebels' perimeter, but the rebels would then close in behind and effectively cut it off.[53] Still, despite his successes, Barzani played a cautious game and made no attempt to form an independent state. The Iraqi government held the major cities—as-Sulaymaniyah, Kirkuk, and Mosul, but the situation was fluid. The Barzanis invaded the outskirts of the towns and entered them under cover of night. To all intents and purposes, at the end of 1962 and the beginning of 1963, the Kurdish northern area had reverted to the wild condition of almost complete anarchy that had prevailed between the two world wars. Meanwhile, in Baghdad events were in motion to bring about a political solution to the rebellion.

The First Baathist Regime

In December 1962, Arab nationalist student members of the Baath party at the University of Baghdad went on strike to protest the inadequacy of the Kassem regime. Kassem put down this mild insurrection easily, but afterward, he began a purge of suspected Baathists in the army,[54] and in February 1963, he retired fifty-eight officers who had Baathist ties. Earlier, he had retired a former head of police, Taher Yahia, a Baathist who, on his own, had been developing contacts with the KDP, which was then operating underground.[55] Now, just before a coup, an arrangement of sorts was worked out whereby the Baath party agreed to support Kurdish aspirations for autonomy and in return, the Kurds would stop pressuring the Iraqi military machine in the north. This arrangement would give the Baathists a respite so they could concentrate on overthrowing Kassem.[56]

The Baath coup came on February 8, 1963. Large elements of the military were committed although Kassem had his defenders, in particular his palace guard, who held out with him. But ultimately he and his people were overwhelmed, and he was executed.

When the smoke had cleared, Abdul Salem Aref, an early opponent of Kassem (who had jailed Aref in the early days of his regime and had once condemned him to death), emerged as the coup's leader. But standing behind him and providing most of the fire and direction were the young officers of the Baath party. And young they were—many of them being barely out of high school. These young officers immediately set about repaying old scores, particularly against the Communists who had savagely persecuted the Arab nationalists at Mosul and Kirkuk. The Baathists formed their own militia, a so-called national guard, which roamed the major cities of Iraq unleashing orgies of vengeance. Through all the upheaval, the Kurds waited. Having ingratiated themselves with the Baathists by opening conspiratorial negotiations prior to the coup, the Kurds awaited the payoff that they assumed was assured.

However, when formal negotiations between the two groups began in the spring of 1963, it was obvious that the parties were miles apart in their positions. Autonomy, as the Kurds defined it, must include

1. formation of a Kurdish provincial executive and legislative council and a vice-president elected by Kurds to sit with the president of the republic in Baghdad;
2. creation of Kurdish security forces in the form of a Kurdish division or "legion" to be stationed in Kurdistan, although under Baghdad command; also, some form of Kurdish provincial police, whose status would be similar to that of a state police in the United States;
3. withdrawal of non-Kurdish units of the Iraqi army from Kurdish territory except as accepted by the Kurdish provincial executive and legislative council or in time of war or danger of war;

4. the spending of a fair share of state revenues (mainly oil royalties) in Kurdistan;
5. appointment of Kurds to all official posts in Kurdistan; and the recognition of Kurdish as an official language, in addition to Arabic, in Kurdistan.[57]

The Baathists were taken aback by the terms the Kurds presented. The former described their vision of future Arab-Kurdish cooperation as "decentralization," a term that was never explicitly defined as its meaning was to be worked out after consultations. The government issued a statement on March 9, 1963.

> Since one of the main aims of the Revolution of Ramadan 14 [February 8] is to establish a modern system based on the best administrative and governmental methods, and since the method of decentralization has proved to be beneficial, therefore, the Revolution, acting on the basis of the revolutionary principals announced in its first communique providing for strengthening of Arab-Kurdish brotherhood and for respect of the rights of Kurds and other minorities, approves the national rights of the Kurdish people on the basis of decentralization. This should be entered in the provisional and the permanent constitutions when they are enacted. A committee will be formed to lay down the broad lines of decentralization.[58]

The Kurds seem to have been motivated to present their stiff demands by the initiation in 1963 of union-discussions between the Iraqi and Syrian Baath parties and Nasser in Egypt. A union between Egypt and Baathist-dominated Syria had just collapsed in September 1961, but afterward there had been a coup in Syria, and a new wing of the Baath party had come to power there. The Baathists now had taken power in Iraq, and it seemed worthwhile to make another attempt at union. Nasser, however, saw that what these young Baathist officers really craved was legitimization. They were nobodies, and they had no way of commanding popular allegiance. Nasser, whose leadership role was assured in the Arab Middle East, could confer legitimacy on these arrivistes.[59] However, in 1963, Nasser rejected any union that was less than complete. He would support a union of Egyptian, Syrian, and Iraqi people, but he would not accept union between Egypt and the Syrian and Iraqi Baath parties (because, clearly, he would be outvoted two to one).[60] The unity discussions, held in Cairo, foundered, but the fact that they were held at all disturbed the Kurds.

When Aref and the Iraqi Baathist officers returned from Cairo empty-handed, they affected a union of sorts with the Syrian Baathists. Mainly, they merged their military commands, and a Syrian brigade was later assigned to duty in Iraq. Aref and the Baathists dealt with the Kurdish question by downplaying it for a while. Then, in June 1963, Aref delivered an ultimatum: The Kurds had twenty-four hours to lay down their arms. The war was on again.

The asssault on the Kurds was awful but quite in keeping with the ideological character of the new regime in Baghdad. The most outstanding event was the bulldozing of a Kurdish suburb in Kirkuk. Kinnane describes the Baath assault.

> The Baath offered a £100,000 reward for Mulla Mustafa— dead or alive—and launched an offensive that far surpassed any of Kassem's in ferocity and thoroughness. Iraqi air and ground forces were co-ordinated in the systematic reduction of Kurdish villages and encampments. Christian missionaries later reported in London that Baghdad forces had surrounded a number of villages, penning the populations inside, and then destroyed the villages house by house using artillery and aircraft. It was also reported that on 13 June an Iraqi unit used a shield of Kurdish women and children to cover its advance. When rebels opened fire after the non-combatants had passed, Iraqi tanks ran down the women and children. Many thousands of Kurds were transported from their homes in the Kirkuk area to farther south in Iraq.[61]

On the military front, the Iraqi army moved forthrightly against the Kurds, this time with the assistance of a Syrian brigade. The Kurds reverted to their favorite tactic of relinquishing ground rather than allowing themselves to be trapped. But this time the ferocity of the Baathist advance was such that in a short time, the Kurds found themselves crowded close to the Turkish and Iranian borders. Two things happened now: The Turks and Iranians conspired with the Baathists to finish off the Kurds once and for all, and the Russians, getting wind of Operation Tiger, as it was called, warned the three groups that the Soviet Union would not tolerate the genocidal destruction of the Kurdish people.[62] The Soviets, reacting against the Baathist destruction of the Iraqi Communists and favoring the Kurds, who had then welcomed the Communists to the north to join the fight against Baghdad, went further. In May 1963, the People's Republic of Outer Mongolia, acting at the USSR's behest, requested a UN session on the alleged Iraqi genocide against the Kurds. Nothing much came of this proposal, however, and it was subsequently withdrawn, probably because the USSR did not want to antagonize 110 million Arabs.[63]

Winter was now coming and the Iraqi army was attempting to push an all-out drive against the Kurds. Mulla Mustafa Barzani, the KDP, and the detribalized forces were fighting on sheer nerve and instinct. Nothing less than survival was at stake.

The winters in the north of Iraq are terrible and can dampen the wildest ideological zeal. Ultimately, the Baathist advance faltered, and the Kurdish line stiffened. Then, in November 1963, Aref, who had promoted himself to field marshal, engineered a deft coup that neatly extruded the Baathists from power. What Aref seems to have been reacting against in Iraq was nothing less than a complete talent drain. Since 1958, all of the contending forces in Iraq had been fiercely dedicating themselves to wiping each other out. What was left in 1963 was one man, Aref, and, as Khadduri puts it, the collection of inept schoolboys that constituted the Baath party.

Teachers from neighboring Arab countries were recruited to fill some [school posts] while Iraqi educators were either serving terms in prison or fled the country to teach in Kuwait, Libya, Saudi Arabia or elsewhere. No wonder that after the Ramadan [Baathist] revolt the standard of efficiency in the bureaucracy continued the decline which had already been keenly felt since the July Revolution. The Baath Party tried to infuse new blood in the administration by the appointment of its leading members in high posts, but most Baathists were very young—some of them had hardly yet completed high school—obviously lacked experience and could scarcely contribute to the improvement of a bureaucracy that had been drained of experienced administrators.[64]

The Iraqi state simply could not continue to function under this inept management. Had the Baathists been able to suppress the Kurds completely, the resulting glory might have enabled them to maintain themselves in power. But once the Baathist advance faltered, popular resentment made itself felt, and Aref, the opportunist, acted to call off the war with the Kurds and eject the Baathists. The second offensive against the Iraqi Kurds had ended, and a cease-fire took effect in January 1964. But this time, a different spirit prevailed among the Kurds. Mulla Mustafa had survived the Baathist onslaught, but he had been badly shaken by it—some even said he had lost his nerve.[65]

The period of Abdul Salem Aref's rule—from November 1963 to April 1966—gave the Kurds a respite from fighting since practically the whole of the period was marked by intervals of negotiations and was only barely disturbed by violence. Aref was not an ideologue, as the zealous young men of the Baath party had been. Early on in his rule, he did try to put into practice some of the Baathist's extremist policies by nationalizing various industries, but when the nationalizations proved unpopular, he reversed his policy. He replaced his prime minister with Abdur Rahman Bazzaz, the first civilian head of government since the 1958 revolution. Bazzaz promised to introduce "prudent socialism," a euphemism for returning the country to private enterprise. The West responded immediately; the USSR and Nasser were expectedly upset, and the Iraqi military also opposed Bazzaz, mistrusting him because he was a civilian.

Perhaps to placate the military, President Aref agreed to launch yet another offensive against the Kurds in 1966. That offensive was set for April, but it was aborted when Aref died accidentally in a helicopter crash. Abdul Salem's brother, Abdur Rahman Aref, succeeded him and ordered the invasion that began in May 1966. It lasted a month and was an immediate disaster for the Iraqis, who lost almost 2,000 men when the Kurds cut off a whole army brigade at Mount Handrin in Kurdistan. Prime Minister Bazzaz then announced—with President Aref's blessing—a twelve-point program for a peaceful solution of the Kurdish problem.[66]

The twelve-point program functions for the Kurds and the Iraqis as Resolution 242 does for the Israelis and the Arabs. Both sides profess to find fault with it, but it is the only basis on which to establish peace should serious negotiations ever be held. Unfortunately for the Kurds, the military acted yet again to check the premier. They brought pressure on Aref to make Bazzaz resign, and shortly afterward, Aref himself was replaced in a bloodless coup. This coup, which took place in June 1968, returned the Baath party to power, the same party that had tried to destroy the Kurds in 1963.

7
An Assessment of the Crisis

In January 1964, after Aref had, in effect, overthrown his own government by turning on his Baathist colleagues, Mulla Mustafa Barzani agreed to a cease-fire. This truce occasioned widespread consternation when it was revealed that Barzani got next to nothing in return for agreeing to rein in the Kurdish forces. Dana Adams Schmidt, a strong supporter of the Kurds, expresses amazement that "after 29 months of intermittent fighting and suffering [Barzani] could have agreed to a deal like that."[1] But the Kurds' situation was to grow even more surprising, for in six months, a fundamental split had opened in Kurdish ranks that pitted Barzani against the KDP leadership. Actual shooting exchanges erupted, and in August 1964, the KDP was driven into exile in Iran by the Barzanis.

To understand this strange change of fortune it is necessary to investigate the events of those days on two levels, international and internal, the latter relating to matters affecting Barzani's dealings with the KDP and to the antagonism of the tribes toward that organization. This chapter reexamines the complex events detailed in Chapter 6 from the conflicting viewpoints of the KDP and Barzani and offers an assessment of the split in the Kurdish nationalist movement.

As a journalist, I interviewed the KDP leaders in Tehran in 1964 after they had been driven out of Iraq by Barzani. I then traveled to Raniyah in northern Iraq where I interviewed Barzani about the party's expulsion. Both versions are presented here, and then I attempt to discern who was right or where the greatest justification lies.

The Party's Version of the Break

When word of the Barzani-Aref cease-fire of January 1964 reached Ibrahim Ahmad, secretary-general of the KDP, he was in Europe on an arms-buying mission with another KDP member, Aziz Shamzini. The cease-fire was announced on February 10 and was greeted by Ahmad and Shamzini with pleasure, "because like everyone else in the world we felt that a cease-fire must be followed by negotiations—terms to strengthen and advance our victorious revolution."[2]

Ahmad and Shamzini returned to Iraq and saw Barzani in Qal'at Dizah, just west of Sar Dasht, at the beginning of March. According to Ahmad, Barzani told him that the liberated areas were to be handed back to the government and that the Kurdish fighters were to lay down their arms and return to their homes. This was the aspect of the cease-fire that had so astounded Schmidt when he first learned of it in an interview with Aref. "No, no negotiations!" Aref told the reporter Schmidt, "There is no need for negotiations, no discussions."[3] It seemed, writes Schmidt, that Aref was playing the role of the "'Great White Father,' generously dispensing justice in measured doses.... [he] could not bear the idea of dealing with the Kurds as equals."[3]

Ahmad's version of the interview in which the two KDP officials reproached Barzani for his action, as he related it to me, is as follows.

> Mulla Mustafa spoke to us about the terms of the cease-fire. He confirmed all the rumors that the liberated areas must be given back, and the partisans must be sent home. Mulla Mustafa said, "The government does not permit the existence of the party in Iraq."
> I said, "Why did you accept such an agreement with a government on the verge of death?"

In February 1964, the government was very weak—even Arab soldiers were running to our side. They were tired and afraid.

Mulla Mustafa said, "Our people are tired."

We said, "Our people are no more tired than the government forces. Ask the man who's lost a house, a brother. Ask this gentleman, he will say: 'I was the owner of a house and farm, a living wife, a brother. It was an honest life—only it was subject to the Arabs. I lost my wife, my brother, my farm. Of what shall I be tired now?'"

At this point, Barzani's argument took a different tack. "He claimed," said Ahmad, "that he was told not to hit the government so hard. An external power desired the government to remain." That power, it appeared, was the United States. I pressed Ahmad for more information about this alleged intervention by the United States, but he knew no more about the affair than what Barzani had told him. Barzani had been adamant that the United States wished a respite in the fighting; it was worthwhile to accommodate such a strong power, which Barzani had done. Ahmad and Shamzini had withdrawn, neither convinced of the wisdom of the strategy their leader was following.

In April, the KDP called a party conference, attended by the members of its central committee and Politburo, at the party's headquarters in Mawat close to the Iranian border. This conference formally condemned steps taken by Mulla Mustafa. It is difficult to see the worth of this condemnation, for the party leaders did not have the influence to dissuade Mulla Mustafa from proceeding on the path he had chosen, nor could they force him to act against his will. Ahmad claimed that moral suasion ultimately would bring Barzani around—because, having accepted the cease-fire, he had to produce results, but the KDP leaders felt certain no results would be forthcoming. The people, however, expected to hear the outcome of their long struggle, and they were becoming more and more restive. The KDP, by dissociating itself from the agreement, hoped to confirm the people's fears that there had been a sellout and thus force Mulla Mustafa's hand.

In May 1964, the new government of Taher Yahia (the prime minister under Aref, who remained president) announced its provisional constitution for Iraq in which there was no specific mention of rights for the Kurdish people; rather, it spoke of guarantees for the Kurdish nation within the Iraqi national unity. This phrasing greatly antagonized the KDP because, said Ahmad, "if we are a *people,* then they must give us our land." The Kurds' essential argument reproduced that of the Palestinians and, indeed, of any people that has sought to claim the right of self-determination: Peoplehood equals land.

The promulgation of the new provisional constitution, with its glaring deficiencies, compromised Barzani to the extent that at the end of May, he made overtures to the KDP to meet with him at his headquarters at Raniyah.[4] Ahmad and Telebani traveled to Mulla Mustafa's camp, arriving at the same time as a delegation from Baghdad, which included Prime Minister Taher Yahia, the commander of the second Division, the director of army intelligence, two or three ministers, and the governor of as-Sulaymaniyah.

Ahmad claimed that this meeting was staged by Barzani to put the KDP in a bad light. Barzani is supposed to have played a part that was demure—Ahmad claimed the meeting opened with Barzani demanding that the government officials give him a visa so he could go to Iran. Asked to explain why, Barzani replied: "Because the government is not helping me. It's better I leave." Barzani was placated and consented to remain, but he refused to participate in the discussion. To all questions put to him, he answered: "There are the representatives of the tribes and party. You speak to them." From that point on, all discussion was between Yahia, the government representative, Ahmad, Telebani, and the tribal representatives.[5]

The point of immediate contention was the language of the provisional constitution. Ahmad and Telebani insisted some reference be made to the Kurdish people—"otherwise we could be thought of as a tribe. When you say we are a people you have to give us our land. There are tens of thousands of Assyrians—but they have no land." Yahia agreed to change the wording of the constitution to include a specific reference to the Kurdish people, but he insisted that final determination of precisely what rights might be claimed by the Kurds must be left to the Iraqi parliament (none had been formed since the 1958 revolution). This stand begged the question of what would be done for the Kurds in the interim.

The government delegation offered the Kurds a proportion of the ministerial posts commensurate with their population, other government jobs, and guaranteed opportunities for entrance to college and university. Ahmad and Telebani said this offer was nothing. There must be some concrete expression of the Kurdish people's existence, "that there is a people called Kurds, living in a land called Kurdistan, which is part of Iraq." At this point, the head of security said, "You may cut out my tongue, I will never say Kurdistan," and the meeting threatened to break up. Finally, it was decided that the government delegation would remain another night and that in the morning, the Kurdish side would present specific proposals, which the government might agree to.

During the night, Mulla Mustafa sent a message to the Kurdish delegates (through Salah Yussefi, head of the Kurdish delegation in Baghdad) enjoining them to be firmer. "Don't be so easy," he is supposed to have counseled, "Ask for what you want." In retrospect, Ahmad and Telebani felt Mulla Mustafa was setting them up, and subsequent developments could justify that interpretation.

The Kurdish side agreed that until a final solution could be reached in parliament, they would require an administrative *liwa.* "No political rights. Don't call it Kurdistan. However, the officials of this unit must be Kurds. Give us that, and we agree to everything in the government plan."[6] Ahmad claimed he asked to read this agreement to Mulla Mustafa, who answered, "No, I am with the people."

The following day, the Kurdish delegation read the agreement to the prime minister, who said, "Finally, just now it is proved to me that you [the party] are the enemy of peace in northern Iraq."[7] Ahmad replied, "I don't care how you regard me, as long as I have the faith of the Kurdish people." The prime minister prepared to leave the meeting, saying, "Anyone who accepted such a proposal would be a traitor." Ahmad and Telebani warned that the Politburo was prepared to fight, to which Yahia replied, "You are ten people." "No, we have the support of all the people." The prime minister retorted: "You do not even have the support of Mulla Mustafa. Let us ask him." And Mulla Mustafa answered: "Ask our beloved father, Aref, to give us amnesty. That's all I want."

The government delegation returned to Baghdad. Immediately afterward, Mulla Mustafa gathered all the people who were in Rahiyah—tribesmen, chiefs, army men—and told them that essentially, the government had not given the Kurds a thing. The gathering agreed to send a delegation to Baghdad; Mulla Mustafa agreed, and a committee was set up. Three days later, the Iraqi governor of as-Sulaymaniyah came to Raniyah, and after he left, Barzani announced that he and the governor had agreed on "many things, which will be published soon." Asked why he had not given the governor the draft of a proposal the negotiating committee had formulated, Barzani said: "No need. Everything is settled."

After four days had passed without publication of the results of Barzani's talk with the governor, Kurdish officers began to approach Telebani and Ahmad and acknowledge that Mulla Mustafa's behavior justified suspicion. It was agreed that a Revolutionary Council composed of officers, tribesmen, and party members should be established, with Mulla Mustafa as its head.

The KDP viewed this council as a means of curbing Mulla Mustafa's dictatorial power. How Mulla Mustafa viewed it is not known, but his initial reaction was favorable: He agreed to its creation with himself as its head. Further, he agreed that the dispute between the party and himself must be settled, and it was suggested that a party congress be convened to address these problems. An agreement to resolve differences was signed, and for a brief interval, it appeared that the threatened split between the party and its chief had been averted.

Developments immediately after the Raniyah meeting, however, proved alarming. Ahmad claims to have intercepted a message from Barzani to one of his commanders at Rawanduz informing him of the forthcoming congress and instructing him to send delegates—but none supporting Ahmad "and the betrayers of the Kurdish cause. These men will be expelled." The Politburo concluded on the strength of this one message that others like it had gone out. Therefore it was likely that Mulla Mustafa was stalling merely to gain time, that his mind was set, that "he would smash us." Barzani was beginning to collect adherents in the cities and enrolling them as party members, but they were not party men. As originally set up, the party was a select group; by opening its ranks to just anyone, Barzani was significantly changing its character. There was not much, however, that Ahmad and Telebani and those loyal to them could do but to withdraw to their headquarters at Mawat. Barzani then pressed his campaign against the party from another quarter: With money that Ahmad claims he got from Baghdad, Barzani began suborning party regulars. The Politburo observed these assaults upon the party with increasing dismay.

Meanwhile, more messages from Mulla Mustafa were intercepted that revealed that he had arbitrarily moved up the date of the congress. Previously, he and the Politburo had agreed on August 1, but Mulla Mustafa was now announcing that it would be held at the end of June. In mid-June, Mulla Mustafa left Raniyah for three days—no one knows for where, but Ahmad claims to have gathered information from Baghdad that Mulla Mustafa was negotiating with the government to fight the party.

Ahmad and Telebani decided to send two party members, Ali Abdullah and Aziz Shamzini, to argue with Barzani against the split. The Politburo professed that it was ready to do whatever Barzani wished as long as he would continue the struggle and agree that the party congress be held according to party rules; i.e., that it be attended by party men, not members of the tribes enrolled as party members. Barzani refused to see the party's representatives; instead, he had them arrested, held for six weeks, and then expelled to Iran.

On July 1, Ahmad received a telegram telling him, Telebani, and the rest of the Politburo to be present at the Sixth Congress of the party to be held two days later at Raniyah. The Politburo wired back that this meeting could not be a congress, since the Central Committee, not the president, must convene it. Twelve men came from Mulla Mustafa's congress to Mawat to fetch the Politburo to Raniyah, but the Politburo resolutely refused to budge.

Also in the first week in July, the party decoded a message from the governor of as-Sulaymaniyah to Iraq's defense minister reporting that Mulla Mustafa had given the Politburo its last warning "to come to the right road, otherwise he will fight them." They had until July 10. On July 7, the party intercepted another coded message in which the governor of as-Sulaymaniyah reported giving Mulla Mustafa 30,000 dinars. Later, another message from the governor to the defense minister was intercepted: Lokman, Barzani's son, was asking for bullets that "the operations department promised my father." Some 70,000 bullets for three kinds of rifles were delivered, and shortly after the delivery, Lokman, leading Barzani tribesmen, seized various strategic locations surrounding the party headquarters at Mawat.

The party called upon leading figures among the tribes to mediate. They reasoned that if the party sector were abandoned, one part of the Kurdish front opposed to the Iraqi army would be exposed. The party controlled the southern sector, in places with a combined force of their own and Barzani's men. Also, a three-month supply of material was needed in order to fight. Having to fight Mulla Mustafa would severely impair the Kurds' ability to resist the government.

About 700 to 1,000 party men were surrounded at Mawat. Orders were given not to fight, and as Lokman and his men inched forward, closing the perimeter around the beleaguered forces, the party fell back. "We could not believe that Barzani had reached this low standard," said Telebani. The party men waited for word from the mediators, and by mid-August, they were in despair; at the end of August, they crossed into Iran. When the Iranian army, which awaited them, requested that they surrender their arms, the party decided to go back to Iraq. This move occasioned the first shooting exchange with the Barzanis, which resulted in many casualties. The surviving party men then recrossed the border into Iran and gave up their arms. The rank and file were quartered in an abandoned match factory in Hamadan, northeast of Kermanshah, and Ahmad, Telebani, Shamzini, and other top party men were placed under close observation in Tehran. When I interviewed Ahmad, Telebani, and Shamzini there in October, there were reportedly 300 party rank and file left in Hamadan. The rest had returned to Iraq to rejoin Barzani.

The Politburo leaders had a simple explanation of Barzani's behavior: The most important thing in Kurdish life, as he construed it, was the tribe. His loyalty was to his tribe, and to his brother Ahmad.[8] Said Shamzini: "He was eleven years in the Soviet Union. He lost his morale. The summer of 1963 finished him [the summer of the fiercest, all-out onslaught of the Baathists]. Still, we knew his shortcomings. As long as he kept going along the general line, never mind every stone." For Barzani, according to the exiles, the revolution was his job; in his province there was nothing to cultivate, therefore the revolution was the means whereby Barzani subsisted. At the time of the Barzani-party break, he was receiving 30,000 dinars monthly from the government, and Ahmad and Telebani claimed that even Barzani's fighting tribesmen were being subsidized—there were supposedly 1,500 of Barzani's followers on the government payroll.

On a higher, more abstract, level the idealogues of the KDP argued that Barzani shrewdly foresaw that the continuance of the revolution threatened his—that is, the tribal—way of life. The party men were convinced that the way of the future led to social reform. "Every success of the revolution will be regarded as a success of the party. At the end of the fighting must come planning, the settlement of Kurdish society. He [Barzani] has not the mental ability to solve such problems."

Therefore Barzani's sellout, as the party viewed it, was an eminently practical arrangement for him: He accomplished most of his aims—money and rifles for his tribe were assured him. The party thought differently. To them, the tribes had lost their power. In the area controlled by the party, the *agha*s and shaikhs had been nothing, and the party would not help them. To be sure, it could not afford to confront them head-on, and therefore the question of land reform had been postponed until after the revolution. However, wherever the reforms of Kassem had penetrated the area under party control—wherever the peasants had regained the land—the party had allowed the reforms to stand. Therefore the *agha*s feared and distrusted the party and looked to Mulla Mustafa for protection.

But in the end, the party men were convinced that history was on their side. "The end of their [the tribalists'] time is the time of our reviving," said Ahmad.

Barzani's Version of the Break

As one might imagine, Barzani's version of the split was quite different.[9] He claimed that during all the years of the revolution, in the fighting since Kassem's time, the party did nothing. In fact, he went so far as to say that the KDP men had a "conversation" with the Baathists in which they said they would not commit their forces; in this way, Barzani would absorb the full shock of the Baathists' blows while the party husbanded its strength and waited for its chance to seize power. Barzani claimed that for five months, he continually pressed Ahmad, Telebani, and their colleagues to convene a party congress, but that they refused. He sent two telegrams to them to come to him and dispatched a delegation to bring them to him; they refused. Finally, he asked them to return their arms, printing presses, money, and food. When they refused, he sent his people to take them by force. The fight between the party and Barzani's force started on July 13, and lasted only one or two days before the party retreated. What they could not take with them, they burned, and they broke up the broadcasting station. According to Barzani, only 350 retreated to the Iranian border, and of those, only 180 elected to stay in Hamadan.

As to why the party behaved as it did, Barzani's explanation was also simple: The Party sought only to enhance its own position. It extorted money from the people so that the party leaders could live in style, which they did for four years. Barzani advised them to curb their excesses, and they promised to do so, but they broke their promises. In the end, Barzani's assessment of the party was that it was worthless. He said he had been out of Iraq twelve years (actually eleven years). When he had left for the Soviet Union in the late 1940s, the party had 1,764 members; when he returned, it had 180. At the Sixth Congress of the party held at Raniyah in late July, 761 delegates had attended, each representing twenty-five party members (the implication being that this change had been wrought by Barzani).

Barzani's explanation of why he signed a cease-fire with a government that was "on the verge of death" (as Ahmad described it) was disarmingly straightforward. Essentially, he substantiated Ahmad's claim: He signed it at the behest of an "external power." He also specified exactly which power—the United States. In fact, Barzani indicated that there had been two approaches to him by the United States, both urging cessation of hostilities in favor of negotiations—first, when Kassem fell, and again in September or October 1963, just before the fall of the Baathists. The second time he was urged to think of negotiating because "if you can get anything by negotiations, it would be preferable to do so, rather than persevere in the fighting." To use Barzani's word, the United

States had agreed to be "compassionate" with him if he agreed to the cease-fire. The appeals to go easy on the Baath party came from the United States ambassador in Baghdad via men who were "close to the ambassador." It seemed reasonable to Barzani that the United States would intercede for the Baath party, because, as he understood it, the United States enjoyed "benefits" in the Middle East that it wanted to hold on to, and preserving the Baath party would facilitate this desire. Barzani said he had had no written or direct verbal communication with the U.S. ambassador—his contacts were established through third parties. Also, he had heard the Voice of America editorializing that the Kurds would be well advised to cease fighting and to negotiate instead.

Thus, in October 1964, Barzani expected a move by the United States, feeling that if the United States wanted the war against him to stop, it could bring pressure on President Aref to facilitate the arrangements. It was not, however, as if Barzani were waiting for orders to come down from Washington— nothing as unsubtle and direct as that—but there were ways such matters could be arranged. The United States had to know that time was running out. He, Barzani, wanted a U.S.-imposed solution to the war, but, among the Kurds in October 1964, the prevailing mood was one of pessimism. "A great part of our nation," Barzani explained, "says the United States does not want to do anything for us. Little time remains. More than one-half the population favors renewing fighting."

The Iraqi government had ceased to bargain in good faith, and no committees were conferring about the cease-fire. Barzani, who was given to expressing himself through analogies, likened the Kurds' situation to that of a small child whose parents and elder siblings make it a scapegoat for their own mistakes. Successive governments had come to power in Baghdad, and failing to win wide popular support, they had declared war on the Kurds to draw attention away from their own incompetency.

In October 1964, Barzani characterized the Kurdish revolution as a defensive action and said the Kurds would not fight unless attacked. Indeed, he conveyed the impression of someone who had to demonstrate near-inexhaustible patience lest the world accuse him of lawless conduct. He wanted to obtain the rights of his people by negotiations, and anyway, both sides were "broken financially," he said. The people can financially support fighting for only three months because the Baathists had pursued a scorched-earth policy, which had drained the limited resources of the populace. Further, the war could not proceed without heavy weapons as they were necessary to hold the liberated areas. His solution therefore had been to consolidate his hold over the territory he could hold and to organize it. At the Sixth Congress, laws had been enacted, and the framework of an administrative system had been set up. The Kurds intended to behave as if autonomy had been granted them.

There were considerable drawbacks to this approach. The lack of medical facilities was extreme,[10] and schooling for the Kurdish children was woefully inadequate. In such social welfare areas, the Kurdish "government" could in no way provide what was needed. But, as Barzani viewed matters, there was no alternative to the Kurds' adopting their present course of action. After nearly three years of fighting, Barzani was convinced there was no way to force the Iraqis to give the Kurds their rights.

"We must have outside intervention,"—but Barzani was vague as to what, specifically, in the Kurds' situation would tempt a great power like the United States to intervene. "If the United States does not do anything, there is a minority among us Kurds which does not like the United States. And that minority will grow."[11] Why did he think the United States had resisted becoming involved to date? "Pan-Arabism."[12] But he felt this lack of involvement was short-sighted on the part of the United States since the Arabs would grow more and more powerful and threaten United States interests. If the United States felt that the Kurds would threaten the interests of Iraq's neighbors (a reference to the CENTO powers, Turkey and Iran), it should rest assured that the Kurdish revolutionaries in Iraq had no designs on any of their neighbors' territories.

Barzani did not know how much longer the present stalemate in the north could persist, but he felt that the Iraqi government would suffer sooner than the Kurds. "The present government in Iraq came to power in a coup," he explained, and did not have the support of the people. Unable to solve the Kurdish problem, that government would fall, and another would take its place. But Barzani had no illusions about its successor, for the Arabs, in his view, were constitutionally incapable of resolving the problem. "One group in one room wants a peaceful solution. Another in another room wants war."

In October 1964, Barzani stated that the Kurds demanded an area—including as-Sulaymaniyah, Kirkuk, Irbil, and Mosul[13]—that would constitute a single unit governed by the Kurdish people through their own parliament and cabinet. However, foreign affairs, finance, and defense would still be controlled by the ministries in Baghdad. Significantly, there was no mention of a fair share of the oil revenues or a Kurdish army within the Iraqi army, the two chief stumbling blocks in all previous negotiations.

An Assessment

To assess the contrasting attitudes of the contending parties, one may well begin with the KDP cadre—Ahmad, Telebani, and the other members of the Politburo who fled to Iran. Their view is easily assimilated by a political scientist, and it breaks down into a neat paradigm. Barzani was a man of the tribes. The land from which he sprang was too primitive to have embraced a market economy—as Ahmad claimed, it was too rough even to farm, and it provided no livelihood. Instead, one lived by raiding and smuggling. The *agha*s, who retained control of tribal demesnes long after tribal organization had broken down, were aware that the revolution had unleashed forces that were inimical to them. Wherever Kassem's land reforms had taken hold in the Kurdish north and the party dominated, the party allowed them to prevail. Further, the party had mobilized detribalized Kurds. It had introduced military discipline, forming a regular army with uniforms and grades, and the men of this army deprecated the tribes: The KDP had a song, "The *agha*s and the beys suck the blood of the workers. Side by side with all workers we fight against the common enemy, the exploiters." The party, then, although it may not have been Marxist, was definitely the arm of the town-bred Kurd, with all of the antagonisms of the townsman for the countryman, whom he naturally both feared and despised.

The young intellectuals of the KDP also had a working plan to overhaul society, which they borrowed from the Communists—if, indeed, elements of the party were not Communists. Long association with the Communists had shown them not only the ideological arguments to use against the "feudalists," but the methods of organization that would prove effective. It was the latter that Barzani probably should have feared most.

Thus Barzani, in short-circuiting the revolution, was opting for the old ways. Added to this backwardness was the man's alleged broken morale. The Politburo was quite emphatic about this: In the summer of 1963, Mulla Mustafa had lost his nerve. In the all-out drive by the Baathists to seize Raniyah, the Barzanis had nearly abandoned their positions.

Barzani's defense of himself, on the other hand, is pragmatic. He was the victim of forces he could not control, both on the internal and international fronts. On the internal front, the Baathists had Barzani outgunned and used the most sophisticated weaponry against him. He lacked any kind of heavy weapon, his heaviest being three-inch and two-inch mortars. (When I was with Barzani he had no ammunition for the former, desperately needed bazookas and grenades, and had only one twenty-five millimeter cannon, but no ammunition for it). The peasants supported the war, but the scorched-earth tactics of the Baathists imposed severe hardships. In August 1963, Schmidt reported in the *New York Times:*

> The Iraqi army appears bent on breaking the Kurds' will to resist by methods of total war. In addition to bombing and machine gunning of some villages . . . crops have been burned. Villagers have been deported to a zone south of Kurdistan. The economic blockade of the north has been imposed more vigorously. As a result by next spring some Kurds may face starvation.[14]

The scorched-earth policy of the Baathists was not mere vengeance-taking; it was a calculated move to deny the revolution the means to exist.

On the international front, the Kurds' situation appeared equally bleak. With the 1964 round of fighting, the United States moved from a position of neutrality—or even benign support of the Kurds—to one of alignment with the Baathists. C. S. Sulzberger, writing in the *New York Times* after the coup of February 1963, in which the Baathists took power, said:

> An initial appraisal shows Iraq's revolution and its implications are not hostile to U.S. interests. Diplomatic ties [between the United States and Iraq] have been swiftly reaffirmed. There seems sure prospect of ending the Kurdish civil war. And Communism, which had been gaining under the un-steady hand of Kassem, has been swatted in the head.[15]

In fact, in response to the Baathists' move away from the Soviet Union, the United States made a corresponding move to reestablish ties with Iraq. The Russians had broken an arms contract for some $400,000,000 in assistance, which the West offered to replace. Britain agreed to supply the Baathists with Hawker-Hunter aircraft, among other items, and the West's allies—Turkey and Iran—agreed to close their borders to the Kurds.

In the Kurdish-Baathist war, then, the United States, Britain, and their allies supported the Baathists. The USSR opposed them along with Nasser, the latter considering the Baathists' war against the Kurds to be pointless—it only drew resources away from the major battle against the Zionists.

In 1964, the Baath regime may have been, as Ahmad described it, a "government on the verge of death," but the situation for the Kurds was not much better. The Russians were doing nothing for them—and, indeed, supply would have been difficult with the Turkish and Iranian borders closed. The second offensive of the Kurdish-Iraqi war had simply ground down, and both sides were financially broken, so Barzani's explanation for the cease-fire makes sense. It is futile to argue whether he did right to accept a truce, but if we accept his view that the Kurds alone could not force a solution to the war, then we must accept the good sense of his decision to quit fighting. The parties to the conflict had effectively neutralized each other, and in 1964, no outside power—with the exception of the Israelis—had an interest in actively intervening on either side of this awkward little war.[16]

The final assessment would have to be that Barzani was right to accept a cease-fire when he could not force a military decision. However, he was wrong to play down the KDP's accomplishments. In fact, the KDP had politicized Kurdish society—something that had not been done previously in history.

The fighting units of the KDP were modeled on the *pysht mala,* the personal bodyguard of the traditional *agha*s. The KDP units styled themselves *pysht merga* (those who were prepared to die), and they performed two essential functions: tax gathering and fighting.

The tax-gathering function of the *pysht merga* represented an attempt to systematize what previously had been indiscriminate looting by the predator tribes. While I was in Kurdistan, I received an account of how the tax-gathering operated. I visited one town, Qal 'at Dizah, that lived off smuggling, like many other towns in Kurdistan. When the

KDP took over Qal 'at Dizah, it allowed the smuggling to be continued, but it taxed the smuggled goods at rates varying from 1 to 5 percent for rugs to 75 percent for alcohol. This taxation brought the KDP about thirty-five dinars a day, enough to support the fifty to sixty *pysht merga* quartered in the town.

The reader may object that there is not a lot of difference between this method of obtaining "loot" and that of the bandits, but the KDP also assumed responsibility for the town of Qal 'at Dizah. The party arbitrated the town's blood feuds, it convened courts at which it heard cases and handed down judgments, and in extreme cases it administered capital punishment. In effect, in the areas under its control, the KDP strove to supplant the tribal organization with an organization of its own.

The KDP's supreme accomplishment, along the lines of creating an organization, was the Revolutionary Council. The party had intended that the council should ultimately rule over an autonomous Kurdistan and that it should replace Barzani's one-man rule with a form of collective leadership.

The party's original plan was that the council should be composed of fifteen elected members—five elected by the party; five, by Barzani; five, by the peasants in every province—two independent personalities, who would be appointed; two Arab officers; and two tribal chiefs. When Barzani vetoed this composition, it was changed—with Barzani's blessing—to forty-three members all told: seventeen party members, ten "force" leaders ("force" was a Kurdish term for a military unit), two priests (representing the Assyrian community), twelve heads of tribes, the Kurds' European representative, and the head of the Kurdish Students Organization in Europe. This council, which was voted into being by the Kurds in October 1964, functioned as a parliament, and it chose from its members an executive bureau, or cabinet, which included ministers of the treasury, interior, foreign relations, tribal liaison, and liaison to the Christian community.

Unfortunately, we have no way of knowing how the council functioned in practice, because it came under control of Barzani almost immediately, and he used it like a rubber stamp. But even so, the creation of the council represented an advance over anything Kurdish society had seen previously. It certainly was an advance over anything produced by the Mahabad Republic, because the Russians had imposed organization there. The council that came into being in 1964 appeared from below. Elements from within the Kurdish nationalist movement wanted to direct the course of the movement.

In 1964, the Kurdish national struggle stood on the brink of being transformed into an authentic war of liberation. A link had been forged between the fighting elements, which prosecuted the war, and the masses who supported them. That link did not last long, but it represents the high point achieved thus far by the Kurds in their political affairs.

8

The Continuing Kurdish Question

In 1964, the Kurdish leadership around Mulla Mustafa Barzani was convinced it had everything to gain by playing a waiting game with the Iraqis. Successive governments had come to power through staged coups, but they had lacked popular support, and the officials in these governments had been inept. As they failed to solve Iraq's social and economic problems, they attacked the Kurds as a way of diverting the people's attention. But that tactic had now been proved futile, and all the Kurds had to do was hold out against the first shock of Baghdad's "all-out" offensive. The winter snows came, and the Iraqi military slunk back into the plains, faced with many problems that were clearly beyond its capacity to deal with. In 1964, the Kurds figured that sooner or later, the Iraqis would have to face the facts: The Kurds were too tough a nut to crack and the government should deal with them.

Of course, the Kurds' strategy was wrong, but for reasons they could not have suspected in 1964. Something happened in 1969 that drastically altered the Arab Iraqis' chances of success in Baghdad.

In that year, then-Major Muammar Qadafi and a phalanx of equally young, untested Libyan officers, overthrew the Libyan regime of King Idris, deprived the Americans of their most forward base in the Middle East, Wheelus, and began to do battle with the foreign oil companies. The coup took place on September 1, 1969; by the summer of 1970, Qadafi and his fellow officers had won a thirty-cent-per-barrel increase

159

in the price of Libya's high-grade oil, an increase that soon was adopted elsewhere in the Middle East.

One of the countries to follow Libya's lead was Iraq. That country's increase, which represented an additional fifty-five cents per barrel the first year, came as a windfall to the Baathists, who had again taken over the government in 1968 and who had, like their predecessors, been bedeviled by seemingly unsolvable economic problems. The increase meant more money to spend on development projects—popularity could, in effect, be bought. No longer need the military men worry about a sullen, mutinous civilian population at their backs while they were paying off old scores in the Kurdish north. This change was just what the Arab officers needed to tip the power balance between the Kurds and them decisively in their favor.

In this chapter, we will look at what led up to the hideous, for the Kurds, major reverse of 1975, the upheaval of that year, and its aftermath. The collapse of the Kurdish revolution was accompanied by considerable commotion, and so much controversy was generated that it is difficult, even at the late date of this writing, to say definitively what happened. Among others, the conspiracy theorists have had their say[1]—claiming that the Kurds were betrayed by a combination of forces including the shah of Iran, Henry Kissinger, and the CIA[2]— and their claims will be discussed.

The Second Baathist Regime in Iraq

In 1968, when the Baath regime returned to power in Iraq, it behaved in a confused manner initially. It advertised itself immediately after the coup of July 17 as slightly right of center,[3] a fact attested to by the presence in the takeover government of two pronounced rightists, Abd al-Rizak al-Nayef and Ibrahim Daoud, and a back-up team of young rightist officers. The government also included some old, moderate leftists, like Hasan al-Bakr, who led the coup. Bakr had figured in the 1963 Baath power-seizure and then had lost to Abdul Salem Aref, the brother of the president replaced in this latest coup (the third successful one in ten years).

Nayef became prime minister (under Bakr, the president), and announced his intention of resolving the Kurdish problem. He invited two Kurds to join his cabinet, but before these selections could be passed on by Barzani (they were in fact Barzani's men), the Nayef government and all the young rightist officers associated with it were whirled away in another coup, this one by Bakr and leftist and pro-Nasser elements. Nayef was arrested and then packed off to an embassy post in Morocco. Daoud, who briefly served as defense minister, was arrested and flown to Rome. Middle East experts now took another reading of the Iraqi situation and pronounced that the government was slightly to the left of center. As was soon to be demonstrated, such a colorless designation could not begin to give a correct description of the forces that finally had taken hold in Iraq.

Iraq in the late 1960s was a sad case among the nations of the Middle East. It had enormous potential resources in its northern region, not only of oil (around Kirkuk) but of water, and hence of electric power, which was already being tapped by the huge dam complex at Darband i-Khan. Iraq had a wheat-growing potential, and its population of some 12 million was not excessive. But despite these advantages, it lagged far behind its neighbor Iran in development. Iraq had never succeeded in tapping the human resources to which it could lay claim, and this fact crippled the country.

Governed in the 1920s by Arab officers, veterans of the Sharifian army who had been in a military school in Turkey and who may have thought of themselves as Turks, Iraq was not a nation for a long time—it was merely the fief of a tight oligarchy that enhanced its own wealth while the mass of Iraqis survived as best they could. I have described in Chapter 6 the bitter—and in many respects horrifying—factional fights that developed when the Hashemite monarchy was overthrown and the resulting reduction in the number of candidates qualified to run the government. It is only with understanding of this background that one can appreciate the activities of the Baathists in 1968.

When Hasan al-Bakr and his left-of-center wing of the Baath party took over in July 1968, they almost immediately unleashed a storm of controversy by announcing the arrest (January 19, 1969) of nineteen "rightist" conspirators[4]—ultimately, sixteen of them were hanged. The essence of the conspiracy, as the Baathists purported to view it, involved attempts by external enemies (most notably Iran and Israel) to frustrate Iraq's participation in the war against the Zionists by tying up its armed forces in successive campaigns against the Kurds. The shah for his part was also alleged to have conspired to raise the Shia of southern Iraq (coreligionists of Shia Iran) against the Baghdad government.

As details of the plot unfolded, it was obvious that it contained elements to offend almost everyone. The Baathists were not only accusing the usual lesser fry, who invariably are caught up in broadly cast intelligence sweeps like this one, but also implicating some of the country's most respected politicians—among them, Abdur Rahman Bazzaz, the civilian premier of Iraq (under the first Aref) who had disappeared and had been believed to be under arrest. Also implicated was Abdel-Aziz Ukaili, former defense minister under the second Aref and a candidate for the presidency when the first Aref died in a helicopter crash. Both of these men were viewed by many prominent Western observers as being among the more "stable" Iraqis.

More startling revelations were made. The Baath regime was accusing the just-deposed president, Aref, of having ties to the CIA,[5] and it was claimed that whole segments of Iraqi society were on that agency's payroll. It was unusual for a government to make allegations of official corruption in such profusion: It is not often that a country's leaders castigate virtually a whole generation of heretofore respected politicians as having been suborned. But the more bizarre elements of the exposé were soon disregarded once it became known that among with nineteen arrested and facing the death penalty were eight Jews. This fact raised the specter—to elements in the West, at least—of pogroms.

An organized campaign got under way to elicit appeals for clemency from UN Secretary-General U Thant, the pope, President Nixon, and the government of France. Even as the appeals were being made, the Baathist government revealed that trials, sentencing, and executions had been completed. Among those executed were ten Jews, which touched off a louder storm of disapproval. In vain did the Baathists argue that Christians and Muslims had also been executed—in other words, that the sentences were not sectarian. To the Baathists the plot was genuine and the aim of the plotters—to deliver Iraq back into the hands of CENTO—was reprehensible. The Baath regime stubbornly kept on with its investigation, and soon more plotters were indicted—among them two Jews— and these, too, were executed. It was reported that thousands of young Iraqi militiamen paraded past the gibbets where the victims' bodies were displayed.[6] The reaction against the events in Iraq continued worldwide.

All this sensational activity might be passed over in silence except for the fact that the events of 1969 are directly related to the revelations of a report issued by the House Select Committee on Intelligence in 1976 (the Pike Report), which alleges that the CIA had supported the Kurdish insurrection.[7] It is therefore worth highlighting the Iraqi charges. Basically, the Iraqi government claimed that the CIA, Israel, and Iran had conspired to weaken the Iraqi government by fomenting rebellion in Kurdistan. The Kurds formed the wrecking crew that rightist elements used to regain power in Iraq, and the rightists, then, were prepared to deliver the country back into the hands of CENTO.

It seemed hardly likely that the Baath regime would attempt a peaceful resolution of the Kurdish problem. And indeed, in January 1969, after receiving a new consignment of weapons from the Soviet Union, the Baathists unleashed yet another offensive in the north. With 60,000 men, this campaign represented the greatest concentration of forces the government had yet dispatched against the Kurds.

Barzani and the *pysht merga* had had ample warning of the assault and were ready for it—as ready as 10,000 men can be to face 60,000. The army struck at Rawanduz and Panjwin in an effort to divide the Kurdish forces in two by slicing directly through Iraqi Kurdistan from Baghdad to Rawanduz. By following the Iranian border, north and south, the army also hoped to effectively surround the guerrillas. The sheer weight of numbers and firepower thrown against the Kurds very nearly defeated them. Strategic towns, like Panjwin and Qal 'at Dizah (which the government had never previously held) fell in short order. Still, as the *pysht merga* were tumbled back toward the Iranian border, they did not succumb to a complete rout but gave ground fighting.[8] This dogged retreat was just enough to fatally compromise the Baathist advance. When February came, the invasion of the north was stalled short of its goal, and Barzani and his guerrillas were still in a position to resist. In the winter, there was not much more the Baathists could hope to accomplish.

As the Baath offensive deflated, the Kurds prepared to receive overtures for a cease-fire—after all, this was the scenario they depended upon. And, indeed, the overtures were forthcoming, and what is more, this time it appeared the Baath regime might finally have learned the lesson previous Arab regimes had resisted. In 1970, the government under Hasan al-Bakr proposed a fifteen-point settlement of the Kurdish problem that was the most far-reaching yet.

The real concessions by the government to the Kurds were these: the appointment of a Kurdish vice-president; the establishment of Kurdish as one of two official languages; and representation for the Kurds in the government, army, police, legislature, and universities in proportion to their numbers. This offer was nothing short of a grant of autonomy, which, in effect, is what the Kurds were demanding.

This disposition of the Baathists to choose peace and negotiation over violence in settling the Kurdish problem was an extraordinary turnabout. Through all of 1969, the Baathists had defied a concerted worldwide campaign against them as they persisted in uncovering internal enemies linked to a subversive Kurdish community in the nation's midst. Now, they were conceding most of what the Kurds were asking for.

One explanation of the change in policy that should be considered is that the Iraqis in 1970 badly needed friends as they had amassed an appalling number of enemies. Witness the fact that Iraq, alone of all the Arab nations that had fought Israel in 1967, had not signed a peace treaty and was therefore technically still at war with "the Zionist entity." Iraq was also feuding with its neighbor, Syria, which was also Baathist controlled, and it may have been Syrian sabotage that damaged the pipeline in 1971 through which Iraqi oil passed to the Mediterranean. That pipeline was not repaired, which ultimately drove the Iraqis to commission the construction of another one through Turkey. To the south, the Iraqis disputed the possession of two small islands at the mouth of the harbor of Umm Qasr, Iraq's port in the Gulf, with Kuwait. The sultan of Muscat was displeased with them also because they had supported rebel secessionists in his territory of Dhofar. Saudi Arabia distrusted Iraq's trafficking with Moscow, but perhaps the most dangerous enemy of all was the shah of Iran.

The Iranian Factor

When the Iraqis appeared ready to negotiate a peaceful end to the Kurdish problem in 1970, the shah warned the United States that such a conclusion played into the hands of the Soviet Union. The shah argued that Iraq was the Trojan horse by means of which the Russians would gain entry to the Gulf—Iraq was, in the shah's eyes, the USSR's agent.[9]

In 1970, Iraq was very much in the Russian camp, and the United States, incriminated as it was in the Arabs' humiliation of 1967, no longer had diplomatic relations with Baghdad. The USSR had benefited from the West's sympathy toward Israel, and, in addition, it had capitalized on the situation.

In 1961, Kassem had nationalized the rich Rumaila oil fields in southern Iraq, when, as he construed it, Western oil companies had failed, for their own corrupt purposes, to exploit the fields to capacity. In order to tap the fields themselves, the Iraqis needed oil technicians, whom the Russians willingly supplied. In 1972, the Baath regime nationalized almost all the remaining Western-controlled oil operation in Iraq (actually, Iraq seized the Kirkuk fields and the pipeline; it did not nationalize the Mosul and Basrah fields). Compensation was paid, but no compensation could reassure the companies that the Iraqis would not now go ahead and "change the traditional trading pattern of Middle East oil"—in other words, abrogate existing contracts to supply oil to Western markets and turn instead to the Soviet Union and the Eastern bloc.[10]

In addition to making oil-related deals with the Russians, the Iraqis also armed themselves with Russian-supplied weapons, buying the latest available T-54, T-55, and TU-22 bombers, Sukhoi-20 ground attack fighters, and MiG-23s.[11] With some 1,000 Russian oil technicians in the oil fields[12] and another 8,000 military "consultants" attached to the army,[13] the USSR's hold on the country appeared solid.

In February 1972, Vice President Saddam Hussein, later to become president after Bakr, traveled to Moscow to conclude military and economic arrangements. The Western press reported that a treaty between Iraq and the Soviet Union was contemplated, as indeed it was. On April 10, 1972, Iraq followed Egypt and signed a fifteen-year friendship treaty with the USSR.

In 1972, then, it seemed to some that Iraq was practically a satellite of the Soviet Union, and the shah of Iran's repeated warnings that Iraq was a Trojan horse seemed to be borne out. It remains to be determined whether the shah had merely been the one to alert the West to this threat, or whether he had in fact driven Iraq into the Russians' arms. This question brings us to an examination of the Iran-Iraq rivalry in the years leading up to 1976, the period in which congressional investigators claim, in the Pike Report, that the CIA aided the Kurds.

In 1972, at approximately the same time that Aleksei Kosygin went to Baghdad to sign the friendship treaty, President Nixon traveled to Tehran where the shah persuaded him to support the Kurdish rebellion against Iraq. In 1972, the rebellion had technically been resolved—Barzani had accepted the Baathists' fifteen-point proposal for ending that dispute—but it remained a live issue because, as so often had been the case with such deals, the government had reneged on crucial points.

Barzani had refused to propose his candidate for the Kurdish vice-president of Iraq until the Baath regime named the governors of the provinces to be included in the Kurdish area. The Baathists, however, balked at appointing a governor for the province of Kirkuk, because since Kirkuk was the source of 65 percent of Iraq's oil, the government preferred not to include it in Kurdistan. A referendum on this point had been part of the 1970 fifteen-point solution, but the Baath regime proposed to base the decision on the 1957 census. Since that census, however, the population of Kirkuk had swelled—as indeed had all of Kurdistan—with Kurdish immigrants, many from Turkey and Iran.

The shah proposed to President Nixon that with a little prodding, it should be possible to incite the Kurds over the Kirkuk issue. It is not known what arguments he used, although one would assume that he emphasized the conclusion of the friendship treaty with Moscow, the Baathists' plans to legalize the Iraqi Communist party and take it into a government coalition, and the fact that reportedly, the Iraqis were going to grant the Russians port facilities at Basrah. These points probably provided arguments enough.

In 1972, Nixon went over the heads of his top intelligence advisors, overrode the objections of the CIA, and outflanked the State Department to order operations supporting the Kurds. It was subsequently revealed that a U.S. commitment was essential to interest the Kurds in restarting the war—Barzani did not trust the shah's word alone. According to the Pike Report, "documents made available to the Committee indicate that the U.S. acted in effect as guarantor that the [Kurds] would not be summarily dropped by the [Shah]."[14]

The United States does not seem to have given the Kurds a great deal: only $16 million,[15] mostly in the form of ammunition (some millions of rounds) with some Russian and Chinese small arms drawn perhaps from stocks held by the Israelis as a result of the 1967 war.[16] The shah was prepared to supply the bulk of Mulla Mustafa's needs; the U.S. share was a token, merely an earnest of the U.S. government's interest in the Kurds' hopes for autonomy.

To some people, it may seem extraordinarily irresponsible of Barzani to have engaged in arms trafficking with the shah and the Americans when he appeared to be on the point of effecting a solution of his over-a-decade-old dispute with Baghdad, but certain Baathist acts, perpetrated in this interval, may have led Barzani to make his deal with the West. Between 1970, when the Baathists first suggested their autonomy plan, and 1974, when they unilaterally enacted the plan, two attempts were made on Barzani's life. Both came close to succeeding, and both could probably be laid at the door of the Baath regime. In addition, the Baath government instituted a policy as early as 1970 of resettling the Kurdish region, concentrating its efforts on Kirkuk. Of this policy Ismet Sherif Vanly writes, "The KDP could not ignore the fact that the policy of Arabization was in force during the transition period (1970–1974), not only in Kirkuk but also in Khanaqin, in the Kurdish districts of Mosul . . . as well as in areas of Arab Iraq settled by Kurds."[17] And finally, from the Kurds' point of view, the Baathists' autonomy proposal had no teeth.

Originally, the KDP and the Baath government had agreed on a proportionate number of seats in the Iraqi parliament for the Kurds, but as late as 1974, Iraq had no parliament— it was still ruled by a Revolutionary Command Council made up of military officers—and it had no permanent constitution.

The Baath regime did create an assembly for the Kurdish region, but the government appointed all the members. This assembly, with eighty members, met in October 1974 in Irbil, but without any real power, it performed no autonomous function.

From the earliest days of the war, Barzani and the KDP had insisted that they were fighting not only for autonomy but also for democracy in Iraq. This assertion was more than rhetoric, for without the introduction of some kind of democratic arrangements, the Kurds could have no guarantee they would retain the gains they had achieved.

After the 1973 war with Israel, the Baath regime delivered an ultimatum to Barzani to accept the fifteen-point plan. When Barzani again raised the issue of Kirkuk, the government mounted an all-out drive against him in March 1974. Allan Holden, writing in the *Sunday Times,* called it the greatest effort by the Iraqi government to that time. The Baathists committed the largest force and the most sophisticated equipment ever, and the fighting was on a scale that dwarfed previous efforts. The drive was spectacularly successful as such operations go. The army found itself in September in possession of more Kurdish territory than it had ever held before, and both Panjwin and Rawanduz were taken. The Kurds fought hard, but this time, unlike all previous times, civilians fled the area, crossing the Iraq-Iran border at the rate of 30,000 a day.[18] By January 1974, the number of Kurdish civilians being cared for in twelve refugee camps was over 200,000,[19] and the number was expected to climb to 500,000. A member of a volunteer medical team of French doctors, *Medecins sans frontieres,* described the condition of the refugees: "Whole families wait . . . with only their baggage and some blankets. . . . Many are reluctant to leave Iraqi territory . . . and have done what little they can to camp in villages . . . Tuberculosis, typhoid, meningitis are all prevalent."[20]

The Pike Report includes an excerpt from a 1972 report by the CIA chief-of-station in Tehran: "The CIA had early information which suggested that our ally [the Shah] would abandon the [Kurds] the minute he came to an agreement with his enemy over border disputes."[21] Two basic border disputes kept the Iraqis and Iranians at odds: one dispute over territories in the central border region and another over the Shatt al-Arab, the waterway that forms Iraq's major entry to the Gulf. These disputes were bitter and long standing, and the Kurds had no reason to believe either could be resolved. Nevertheless, on March 7, 1975, at an OPEC conference in Algiers, the Iraqis and Iranians agreed to a plan that would settle all outstanding differences between the two governments.

The deal struck by the shah with Saddam Hussein (now the effective ruler of Iraq, having taken over from the ailing Bakr) is one of the great surprises of Middle East politics in the post–World War II era. It certainly caught Barzani off guard; there was no time for him to protest. With alacrity, which the Pike Report describes as surprising, Iran shut off border traffic. In fact, "the cut-off came as a severe shock to [the Kurds'] leadership . . . the representatives [of the shah] told them in bluntest imaginable terms that the border was being closed to all, repeat all movement."[22] The report describes the alternatives extended to Barzani.

> He could expect no more assistance from Iran [and therefore] should settle with [Iraq] on whatever terms he could get [meanwhile] his military units would be allowed to take refuge in Iran only in small groups and only if they surrendered their arms.[23]

The Kurds reacted as may be expected, with pain and hurt. The report is particularly poignant on this point as it quotes excerpts from Barzani's cables to Kissinger appealing for intervention: "Our movement and people are being destroyed. . . . We feel your excellency that the United States has a moral and political responsibility toward our people."[24] When the CIA chief-of-station in Tehran cabled Washington urging *some* response from Kissinger to Barzani's importuning, a "high government official" (presumably Kissinger) is supposed to have rejected further involvement of the United States with the Kurds on the grounds that "secret service operations are not missionary work."[25]

At the end of March, Barzani announced that he was surrendering, and on March 30, 1975, he and his son Idris crossed the border into Iran. The Kurdish-Iraqi war had ended with an unequivocal Kurdish defeat.

An Assessment of the Kurdish Defeat

The collapse of the Kurdish rebellion has mystified many observers in several aspects, and the behavior of the United States seems particularly inexplicable: It appears to have thrown away a perfectly good resource. To be sure, in years past, the Kurds benefited Moscow, and the United States had, albeit indirectly, supported the earlier Baathist regime against the Kurds. But from 1969 on, with the sensational Baghdad spy trials and the persistent incrimination of the CIA in plots against the Iraqi nation, Washington's relations with Baghdad deteriorated. Economically, the United States could not have welcomed the nationalization of the Iraq Petroleum Company; strategically, it did not want the Soviet fleet anchoring in the Gulf. Politically, the Baathist regime appeared to be one of the most unstable governments anywhere, and its recourse to the tactic of individual assassination seemed to put it quite outside the bounds of civilized dealings.[26]

History will have the final say on U.S.-Kurdish dealings, but the record as it stands is far from complete. It is risky to attempt to analyze such matters when material has been leaked by parties who are self-interested, but it may still be worthwhile to point out that nothing in the record to date is inconsistent with the past behavior of other powers in circumstances that were roughly similar. How much did the United States actually lose in this affair—or did it lose at all? C. S. Sulzberger observes that Saddam Hussein was ready— after the successful resolution of the Kurdish dispute—to treat with the United States, and that, indeed, several technology deals were possible.[27] Such arrangements, in fact, were made. An analysis in the financial pages of the *New York Times* speaks of "a development boom fueled by $6 billion in oil wealth. Iraq has embarked on a huge development plan with $84.5 billion in imports in the last year. [Further] the Iraqis have taken a decision to exclude ideology from business. Their approach is pragmatic."[28]

The important word is "pragmatic." Dana Adams Schmidt had described the Baath regime in March 1970 as being a mixture of "socialist zeal, ethnic pride and *pragmatism*."[29] Freed of the Kurdish threat to the north, the regime of Saddam Hussein began to divest itself of some of its closer ties to the USSR, and by 1978, the Iraqis had openly rebuked the Russians by executing twenty-one Communist party members. The Baath party further concluded deals that same year for Boeing transports—three 707s, two 747s, two 727s, and a 737—at a total cost of $300 million. As for oil, the United States' chief interest in Iraq, the Iraqis indicated shortly after the Algiers agreement that they were interested in expanding business with the United States. Iraq was moving to a high-consumption economy, and the oil industry was the key to future development.

With all of this cooperation, it is hard not to draw a parallel with the behavior of the British toward the Assyrians after the massacre at Simel in 1932 or, perhaps more appropriately, that of the British toward the shaikh of Mohammara when he was pressured by Reza Shah. In Iraq and Iran the British betrayed the interests of their clients in return for the preservation of stability, that is, the preservation of British interests in the oil of the region. Similarly, the United States had no need to support a risky adventure in Kurdistan if it could get what it wanted—regional stability—by dealing directly with the Iraqi government.

For both the United States and the Soviet Union, stability in the southern Caucasus and Gulf regions—i.e., preservation of the state system—remains a prime desideratum. At no point, up to 1972, is there any evidence that either of the two superpowers had substantially aided the Kurds. U.S. involvement through the CIA, as described in the Pike Report, developed as a fluke and was discontinued almost as soon as it began. And one can see why it should have been, because what was being threatened was nothing less than a system-destabilizing confrontation. The policies of the USSR and of Britain—and later the United States—were no different than those of the Ottoman Turks and the old shahs of Persia when they used the Kurds as minions to harass each other. The Kurds have functioned as pawns for the major powers for centuries, but in the past, the more sophisticated powers always took care to *use* the Kurds and never allowed themselves to be used by them. A system-destabilizing confrontation in the area would serve the Kurds' interests, not those of any of the world's powers. And so it was perhaps natural that as this confrontation threatened, the Kurds' "supporters" began to rethink their options.

An Analysis by an Informed Kurd

Ismet Sherif Vanly in *People Without a Country*[30] has produced an impressive critique of the last days of the Kurdish "autonomy project." He suggests that Barzani's most culpable act was throwing aside restraint. Once Barzani had a promise of aid from the United States to supplement that already proferred by the shah, he burnt his boats.

The chronology is important here. The Baath regime made its fifteen-point proposal on March 11, 1970, and in it the government pledged to implement an autonomy scheme in the north in four years' time. A referendum was to be conducted within a year to determine the area predominantly settled by Kurds, but that referendum was never held, and because of wrangling between Barzani and the Baath government over it—specifically over what was to be the fate of oil-rich Kirkuk—the implementation of the whole fifteen-point program stalled. In March 1974, the Baath regime, on its own, promulgated an autonomy decree tailored to its specifications, leaving it to Barzani to either accept or reject it. He rejected it, but Vanly makes the point that Barzani need not have rejected it completely. "He could have used a thousand little tricks to draw out the negotiations for as long as possible, building up strength all the time."[31] This observation seems sensible. Barzani's rush to battle must have been a result of his confidence that he would be taken care of by Western interests.

Support for Vanly's argument that Barzani lost all restraint once the U.S. connection was assured comes in an interview Barzani gave to a free-lance journalist in 1974.[32] The interview contained such damning admissions as the Kurdish revolution "would accept arms from Israel if the West advised" and we "would be willing to let foreign oil firms into Kurdistan to exploit the fields." These statements contrast sharply with the Barzani I interviewed in 1964, who was extremely circumspect, and the one interviewed in 1963 by David G. Adamson, who referred to him as "the Delphic Oracle."[33] There were Arabs in Baghdad, Cairo, and elsewhere who were disgusted at the bullheaded insistence with which the Iraqi army pursued its costly "feud" with the Kurds, but after Barzani's interview of April 1974 was published, these sympathizers could not have supported him.

Perhaps the most damning criticism Vanly has to level, however, concerns the structural change that took place in the Kurdish revolution when money enriched it. The Baathists' step of unilaterally proclaiming autonomy on March 11, 1974, set off a wave of immigration to the north by professional Kurds—the more well-to-do and the town-bred intellectuals. The Baathist regime had triggered a similar exodus in 1963, but then, the appearance of the professionals proved a liability for the Kurds in the fighting with the central government. The professionals, by their tithing in the towns, funded the revolution, but professionals living off the revolution were a drain. In 1974, the revolutionaries welcomed the professionals, for they could provide the administrative services the revolution needed. The loss of their financial contribution was thought to be not so important—there was the money from the United States.

It soon became apparent, that the professionals would be wasted. According to Vanly, the ex–civil servants, doctors, lawyers, and others tended to collect in the Shuman Valley in Iraqi Kurdistan. "There these cadres found themselves . . . without work or responsibility appropriate to their aptitudes."[34] In other words, the revolution got, in 1974, the bureaucratic organization it lacked—and desperately required—in 1964, but although bureaus multiplied and status-bearing titles proliferated, most of the work performed by the new adherents was "inappropriate."[35]

In the same way, once the fighting recommenced (in March 1974), the Kurdish leadership squandered its base in the people. The Kurdish guerillas, armed now with the more effective weapons supplied by the Iranians, met the invaders head-on. The result was a mass emigration of Kurdish peasants fleeing the area of fiercest confrontation. This flight was a major contrast to the situation before 1964, when the peasants remained in the mountains and cultivated their fields, thus feeding the revolution even as the contributions of the Kurdish professionals in the cities provided funding. This spurning of the peasants' meager, but up until then adequate, contribution was one result of relying on support from the United States. "Why purchase the peasants' tobacco crop when American cigarettes were in plentiful supply?"[36] When the shah abruptly cut off aid, the revolution had nothing to live on. The people were gone, and the fields were uncultivated.

The last point is the substance of the criticism of Ismet Sherif Vanly, the Kurds' European representative, who carried their case to the United Nations in 1965 and was greatly involved in the struggle through all of its last phase. For Vanly, the sudden infusion of copious amounts of cash into a movement that had lived by its wits until 1970 fatally disoriented the leadership. Yet, it is doubtful whether the outcome of the revolution could have been different even if the leader had behaved impeccably, restrained the sudden growth of the bureaucracy, and maintained a good liaison with the people.

The Oil Factor

It is hard to see how the Kurds could have avoided disaster once the Arab oil embargo was enforced. After 1973, stability in the Gulf became the absolute desideratum of everyone (except perhaps the Israelis), and with enormous profits to be made from the sale of oil, Iraq, the world's fourth largest producer, and Iran, the second largest, could not indulge in the luxury of an ideological dispute over control of the Gulf. Iraq wanted to deepen its port at Umm Qasr to enable it to accommodate supertankers, and all of the Iranian fields were around Abadan on the east bank of the Shatt al-Arab.

A quote from an unnamed diplomat reported in the *New York Times* throws light on the dilemma for the Iraqis and the Iranians. In December 1973, two Iraqi MiGs were shot down over Kurdistan by U.S.-made surface-to-air Hawk missiles, and the Iranian military took credit for the kills. This development was extraordinary for now the war had definitely broadened and threatened to draw in the superpowers. Said the diplomat later, "Suspension of aid [to the Kurds] followed realization the war would become major, raising the possibility of heavy damage to the oil fields."[37] This assessment would seem to be not far off the mark. Once there were fortunes to be made out of oil, the Kurdish war became of negligible usefulness to both Iraq and Iran. Vanly writes that what killed the revolution in the end was the "unholy alliance,"[38] in other words, regional cooperation—something the Kurds had always had to fear—and this alliance between Iran and Iraq was brought about by oil.

The Aftermath of Defeat

After the border was closed and the revolution smothered, the majority of the Kurdish guerillas—roughly 20,000 of them—took advantage of a two-week truce arranged by the shah (apparently his one concession to his erstwhile allies) to flee to Iran where they were disarmed. Other fighters surrendered inside Iraq, among them, Salah Yussefi (who Vanly claims was the one Kurdish leader who had inveighed against accepting the shah's "proposal").[39] A small number fought on, retreating into the deepest valleys of the farthest north, right up against the Turkish border. The major gain, if not for the revolution then for the Kurdish people, was that so many of the civilians were able to escape. Before the revolt collapsed, an estimated 500,000 Kurdish refugees had made their way across the border and were housed in Red Lion and Sun camps (refugee camps operated by the Iranian Red Cross). Eyewitnesses attest that these refugees were practically all women, children, and the aged[40]—the able-bodied men had remained behind to fight. When the end was announced, many of these refugees rushed back to Iraq to reclaim their homes; others lingered in the camps. However, eventually all either accepted offers of the Iranian government to relocate in Iran or returned to Iraq. Some known Communists and other people wanted specifically by the Iraqi government were forcibly repatriated. But the fortunate aspect, which may have far-reaching effects for the Kurdish struggle, is that so many civilians escaped and were cared for in exile until they could return or establish themselves elsewhere.

In Iraq, the government initiated an active policy of Arabization of former Kurdish territory, but the autonomy decree still stands. There *is* an autonomous region of Kurdistan in Iraq today, and in that sense, the Kurdish struggle in Iraq did not end as dismally as in Turkey, where the government refuses even to acknowledge the existence of Kurds (referring to them always as "mountain Turks"). However, the area is considerably smaller than what the Kurds agitated for. The provinces making up the autonomous region include: as-Sulaymaniyah, Irbil, and Dohuk, all on the Iranian and Turkish borders—in other words, the most primitive region. Not only has Kirkuk been excepted from Iraqi Kurdistan, but the government also actively carried on population exchanges, removing Kurds and Turkomans from that region and resettling them in the south.[41]

The Reversal of Kurdish Fortunes

After the debacle of 1975, three dates mark an extraordinary reversal of the Kurds' fortunes: February 1979, when the Ayatollah Khomeini assumed power in Iran following the enforced exile of the shah; December 1979, when the USSR invaded Afghanistan; and September 1980, when Iraq invaded the Iranian province of Khuzestan. These events, combined with the long-standing underground war in Turkey, have had the effect of a revolution—erupting in Iran, leaping over borders east and west, and setting the whole region aflame.

The Iranian Revolution

For Kurdish nationalists, the revolution in Iran, which produced the Islamic Republic, renewed dashed hopes. Just after the refugees from Iraq had been resettled (and just after the old guerrilla leader Barzani had died in Walter Reed Hospital in Washington, D.C.), the Kurdish revolt flared again in Iran. Three weeks after Khomeini took power, Kurds seized the army barracks at Mahabad, the site of the Kurds' tragic, lost republic. Khomeini invited the spiritual leader of the Mahabad Kurdish community, Shaikh Ezzedin Hosseini, to parley with him in Tehran, but Shaikh Hosseini refused. Instead, Daryoush Farouhan, the newly-appointed minister of labor, traveled to Mahabad, where Shaikh Hosseini presented him with an eight-point proposal for autonomy—Minister Farouhan found the proposal "harsh."[42]

The Mahabad incident was merely a warm-up, and on March 20, 1979, the Kurds in Sanandaj, the capital of the Iranian province of Kurdistan, followed their compatriots' example. Because Hojjatoleslam Safdari, the Shia religious leader in charge of the the Sanandaj barracks, had refused to give the Kurds arms, they surrounded the barracks and seized the headquarters of the Revolutionary Guards and the radio station, killing an indeterminate number of loyalists.[43]

There were 120,000 Kurds in Sanandaj, and they held 2,000 soldiers penned up in the barracks. Ultimately, another emissary from Tehran, Ayatollah Teleghani, negotiated the soldiers' release in return for certain concessions: A Kurd, Ibrahim Yunes, was appointed governor of Kurdistan; power to appoint security forces in the province was invested in a committee of Kurds, which also had power to oversee the provincial administration, and Kurdish was to be taught in the schools. Considering the concessions granted, one could say that the Iranian Kurds, despite their long oppression under the Pahlavis, had retained a degree of political astuteness.

After the twin incidents of Mahabad and Sanandaj, the international press initially claimed that the Kurds' spiritual leader, Ezzedin Hosseini, a Sunni Muslim, represented the Kurds, but the revolt in Kurdistan actually ran the entire spectrum of political colorings. There was the Iranian KDP, which many of the older revolutionaries rallied to. Their career after Mahabad had been particularly grim, because Barzani, anxious not to offend the shah (and thereby close the friendly border at his back) had renounced all connection with the Iranian Kurdish movement, and in specific instances he may even have cooperated with Savak (the Iranian secret police) to achieve its suppression. Thus, when the Iranian KDP emerged in 1978, it resembled the original KDP in Iraq both in its antipathy to the memory of Barzani and in the leftist orientation of its leadership. The other major faction among the Iranian Kurds that was prominent in the earliest days of the revolt was not specifically nationalist at all: the Fedayeen al Khalq, a Marxist group that had cooperated with the Kurdish nationalists long before the shah's overthrow.

These groups were obviously disparate not only in their political ideology, but also in their generational appeal. Nevertheless, in the early days, all three professed to be able to work in concert. Shaikh Hosseini said, "As a Muslim I don't accept Communism but I accept leftists in our movement because they fought in the revolution against the shah and are fighting for the same thing we are—autonomy."[44]

With so many political groups involved, one would assume that the Kurds' fight was political, but it was touched off by an incident that was rather sordid. After having received, and to a degree absorbed, over 500,000 Kurdish refugees from Iraq, the border area was unsettled. Innumerable weapons had been smuggled into Iran from Iraq and cached—as is the custom in that part of the world—and these weapons were held in readiness for the day when they would be needed. Then, in the last days of the shah's reign and the first of Khomeini's, the price of wheat rose from 8,000 rials to 15,000, which meant that in Iranian Kurdistan, a wheat growing region, there were fortunes to be made. However, Khomeini's people tried to control profiteering—and this action is what touched off the revolt. Cheated, as they believed, of their chance to make a killing, the Kurds went for their weapons.

Nor was the rebellion restricted to Kurdistan as revolts also occurred in the Turkoman territory of the northeast. The land around the city of Gorgan had been much favored by the shah's imperial court, so the shah had parceled out estates there—composed of land belonging to the natives—to his retainers. In February, the Turkoman peasants seized the estates back, plowing the wheat under and setting fire to farm buildings. After the two outbreaks, the message to Khomeini's new regime was stark: Centrifugal forces that had been suppressed in Iran since the beginning of World War II, suddenly released, threatened to tear the country apart. This threat is why, in the first days of 1979, the new regime adopted a conciliatory stance toward its fractious peoples.

Nevertheless, by the end of the summer, Khomeini had branded the KDP as corrupt and as an agent of the United States. These allegations came after the Kurds in Mahabad had boycotted the referendum on Khomeini's Islamic Republic; after Shaikh Hosseini had denounced the election of two non-Kurdish clergymen to represent the Mahabadi Kurds in the parliament as a fraud; and after Abdur Rahman Ghassemlou, now the secretary-general of the KDP, had refused a seat in the Council of Experts, Iran's constitutional assembly. Khomeini declared Ghassemlou's election "null and void," and Ghassemlou responded by accusing Khomeini of "trying to take Iran back to the Middle Ages," which earned him the designation by Khomeini of a "corrupt agent."[45]

By September 1, 1979, Premier Bazargan of Iran had resigned, confessing himself incapable of controlling the revolt in Kurdistan. The same day, Ayatollah Teleghani, who had previously arranged one peace in Kurdistan, accused the Kurds of getting help from the Soviet Union. After that accusation, the Khomeini government opened a full-scale assault on the Kurds.

The tactics the Iranian military used proved—in the short term—quite effective. The Kurdish civilian population was intimidated by jets repeatedly breaking the sound barrier; then helicopter gunships firing rockets and machine guns were introduced. In this way, the government was able to drive the Kurds out of Mahabad and subsequently, Sar Dasht.

Still, Kurdish guerrillas wiped out an army column near the Iraqi border on October 11, 1979.[46] On October 14, they killed the Iranian police chief of Mahabad,[47] and by October 21, they were back in control of the city. This success prompted another reconciliation bid from Khomeini, who promised the Kurds some form of self-rule. This promise may have been an attempt to get the Kurds to vote for the new constitution, but if so, it failed as the Kurdish community again boycotted the voting. Then, in December, there was a major new development.

The Russian Invasion of Afghanistan

In December 1979, the world's attention was turned away from Iran as the Russians invaded Afghanistan, which was no less a shock than the collapse of the shah's regime. To believers in the warm-water-ports theory, the invasion was phenomenal. It appeared as nothing less than a deliberate flouting of Western authority, a direct challenge, and it was treated as such by President Carter, who summarily unveiled the Carter Doctrine, which underscored—as if it had not been plain before—the United States' vital interest in the Gulf.

The Afghans, refusing to knuckle under to the Russians, took to the hills to resist, and in the following month, the Iranian Kurds again began a drive to seize Sanandaj. The world thus had before it the spectacle of two "stans," Afghanistan and Kurdistan, in the grip of proclaimed national liberation movements.

It would appear that both superpowers had been presented with made-to-order situations they could exploit, and yet, the Afghans got very little aid from the United States, and the Kurds got little from the USSR. Neither the Afghans nor the Kurds have been able to acquire sophisticated weaponry of the sort that only the superpowers can supply. Both guerrilla movements have been kept supplied with light weaponry, which enables them to harass their enemies, but in order to escalate their respective struggles, the Kurds and Afghans need rocketry capable of immobilizing helicopter gunships, the scourge of both peoples. By withholding these weapons, the superpowers have kept the Afghan and Kurdish resistance movements in check. Why? In the interest of maintaining stability. In a bipolar world the controlling units will act to preserve what they depend upon, that is, the bipolar system. Direct intervention by either superpower in these regional disturbances would invite a system-destabilizing confrontation. Therefore, except for minor support—funding and the supply of small arms, not to mention all the goodwill in the world—the Kurdish and Afghan liberation movements are on their own. Fortunately for the Kurds, help was on the way—from an unlikely quarter.

The Iraqi Invasion of Iran

By May 1980, the Iranian government and the Kurds had agreed to a cease-fire, which was, in fact, a recognition of a stalemate. In March, the Kurds had repossessed Sanandaj, confining the military garrison to the officers' club while they took over the airport and the television station. The central government had responded by reducing Sanandaj to rubble in a fierce artillery barrage. The Kurds had pulled back to the mountains, and in turn, the Iranians had driven them out of Saqqez, Baneh, and Paveh. Nevertheless, the Kurds had kept control of the roads west of Urmia in western Azerbaijan and had set up an "autonomous republic" there, with municipal councils to administer the region and special police identified by armbands to preserve law and order.[48]

The "liberated" region was now in the hands of a combination of forces, including Ghassemlou's KDP, Hosseini's traditionalists, the Fedayeen al Khalq, and a new group, the Komala (reminiscent of the original Komala of the old Mahabad Republic). It was the Komala, the most radical of the Kurdish groups, that had initiated the fighting in Sanandaj.

That was the situation in June 1980. At the end of the summer, Saddam Hussein, the president of Iraq, ended the 1975 border accord with Iran, Iraqi troops entered Khuzestan, and the Iran-Iraq war was on. The leap of the Iraqis into the fighting came as a surprise to many people who were already dazed by the unexpected events in this part of the world. Again, so close to the event, it is not possible to say definitely what prompted this move, but two factors ought to be considered. Iraq had concluded a peace with Iran in 1975 in order to achieve stability, which both nations had wanted badly so they could cash in on the oil bonanza. Ayatollah Khomeini sought—by all indications—hegemony for Islamic fundamentalists in the Gulf, and he preached revolt to Iraq's huge Shia community (a majority of the population) and also to large Shia communities in Saudi Arabia and other Gulf countries. A Gulf in religious ferment would hardly be stable, so Hussein, in invading Iran—no matter how perverse this statement may appear—was acting to preserve stability.

We must also assume that Hussein believed that the Iranians, with their military machine in ruins, would quickly succumb and that Iraq would therefore get what it wanted, a resettlement of the border question—which, in effect, would have humbled Khomeini. But Hussein badly miscalculated. The Iranians refused to surrender, and by November 1980, the Iraqi offensive was already bogged down. Although the Iraqis held most of the oil-rich Khuzestan province, they could not force a settlement unless they wanted to broaden the war, and if they had gone forward, they would have put great strains on their home front.

Iraq, with a Shia community whose allegiance to the regime was doubtful and with a sullen Kurdish community still smarting from its defeat in the Kurdish-Iraqi war, was in no position to become involved in a larger war in Iran. Instead, the Iraqis pursued a strategy of pushing the battlefront to the northwest, the Kurdish region of Iran. On November 11, 1980, Hussein indirectly threatened to "dismember" Iran by aiding the separatist struggles, not only that of the Kurds, but also those of the Arabs in Khuzestan, the Baluchis, and the Azerbaijanis.[49]

In December, the Iraqi military, which until then had merely been supplying the Kurds, invaded the Marivan district of Iranian Kurdistan, forty miles east of as-Sulaymaniyah, which put Iraqi forces within fifty miles of Sanandaj. All through December, heavy fighting was reported in the area by the Kurds and Iraqis on one side and the Iranians on the other. Certainly, the situation was an anomalous one, with the Iraqis, who had just brutally suppressed a Kurdish insurrection in their own country, supporting Iranian Kurds in their struggle against their central government. Neither the Kurds nor the Iraqis deluded themselves about the situation. An Iraqi officer serving in the Kurdish region told a reporter for the *Christian Science Monitor,* "Here, we have constantly to go around with eyes in the back of our heads."[50]

By April 1981, the Iraq-Kurdish cooperation had grown sufficiently serious for Tehran to offer recognition to all "ethnic rebels" who surrendered their arms,[51] an offer directed mainly at the Kurds. There was no response from Kurdistan. Then

Bani Sadr, Iran's former president, went into hiding from the mullahs, and it was reported that the Kurds had offered him protection. When he escaped from Iran in May, he announced that he had left behind a recently formed National Council of Resistance,[52] which was made up of all groups opposed to Khomeini's rule, including the Kurdish rebels. As of the end of the summer of 1981, there had been no reconciliation of the dispute and the situation remained extremely fluid.

The Situation Today

In 1964, when Barzani drove the KDP Politburo and its supporters out of Iraqi Kurdistan, it appeared that the career of Jelal Telebani was finished. Telebani, however, remained active in the Kurdish national movement, and when Barzani's rebellion collapsed in 1975, Telebani set up headquarters in Damascus where the regime of Hafiz Assad, inimical to the Iraqi Baathists, provided him a base from which to continue the Kurdish resistance. Telebani's group, the Patriotic Union of Kurdistan (PUK), conducted Fedayeen-type raids into Iraq. When the war between Iran and Iraq broke out in September 1980, Telebani's PUK established bases *in* Iraq, in the as-Sulaymaniyah region of southern Kurdistan.

The Iran-Iraq War made allies out of erstwhile enemies; Iraq aided the Iranian Kurdish guerrillas, particularly the Ghassemlou forces. And Telebani, too, found himself cooperating with Baghdad, howbeit indirectly. The weapons that Baghdad supplied to Ghassemlou could be most conveniently conveyed to the Iranian Kurdish chief through the as-Sulaymaniyah region of southern Kurdistan—territory in which the Patriotic Union operated. Telebani agreed to permit units of the Iraqi army to pass through his region in order to deliver weapons to Ghassemlou.

In the summer of 1983 Iran invaded Iraqi Kurdistan in a drive spearheaded by guerrillas of the Iraqi Kurdish Democratic party, Barzani's old party, now headed by his sons, Massoud and Idris. The Iranian thrust into northern Iraq presented

Telebani with a crucial dilemma: Over the years the enmity between himself and the Barzanis had ripened until there was little hope of reconciliation. Telebani felt that he could not ally with the Iranians because to do so he would have had to join forces with his hated enemies, the Barzanis.

Saddam Husayn took advantage of Telebani's predicament by offering to declare a truce with the PUK. Saddam asked Telebani to incorporate his guerrillas into the Iraqi army, where they would form a border guard and defend northern Iraq against the Iranians and the Barzanis. Saddam in return was ready to make a significant grant of autonomy to the Kurds.

Other regimes in Baghdad had proposed truces with the Kurds, often on terms that seemed attractive, but always in the past such agreements had foundered when it came time to work out the details of the negotiated settlement—neither side in the end truly desired, or was in a position to make, genuine concessions. Extenuating circumstances in 1983, however, made it possible for a genuine truce to be negotiated. In the past it had never been in the Iraqi government's interest to permit the formation of Kurdish militias in Iraqi Kurdistan. This was not the case in 1983. Iraq was on the point of being defeated in the Iran-Iraq War. The numerically superior Iranian forces were attacking all along the border, and Iraq's army was nearing exhaustion trying to defend several fronts at once.

Iraq saw an advantage if it reached a settlement with Telebani: The PUK, by agreeing to defend Kurdistan against the Iranians and Barzanis, would free Iraqi army units to confront the regular Iranian forces in the south.

Telebani also saw advantages: He could win limited autonomy for the Kurdish people and, as long as he was permitted to maintain arms, still be in a position to defend himself should Baghdad try to renege on the agreement when and if the Iranian threat was contained. As of this writing, the actual terms of the autonomy offer have not been worked out, but several reliable sources claim that Telebani is insisting that 30 percent of Iraq's oil revenues be spent in Kurdistan.

The first stage of the truce was implemented in January 1984 with an exchange of prisoners between Telebani and Baghdad and with the incorporation of Telebani's PUK into the regular Iraqi army as border guards. This operation has significantly altered the character of the Iran-Iraq War. Now it has become—in the north at least—a war of proxies. Both sides depend heavily on Kurdish surrogate forces—Iraq on Telebani and Ghassemlou; Iran on the Barzanis.

The Saddam Husayn–Telebani arrangement has alarmed the Turks. With a Kurdish population of over 5 million in eastern Anatolia (adjacent to Iraqi Kurdistan) the Turks fear the demonstration effect of Iraq's offer of semi-autonomy to the Kurds. Ankara presently has an active Kurdish separatist movement in its Kurdish areas, where at least ten Kurdish rebel groups operate. The Turks could reasonably complain to both Iran and Iraq that by arming the Kurds they risk destabilizing the whole Turkish-Iraq-Iran triangle.

This appears to be the situation today—traditional Kurdistan is once more aflame and the prospect for the area is increasing anarchy. It seems certain that the various Kurdish groups, once armed, will be almost impossible to manage. The Kurds may cooperate with Baghdad and Tehran for awhile, but in the end, as has always been the case in the past, the Kurds will look out for themselves—which is to say they will resist attempts to reimpose central-government control over Kurdistan, no matter what the outcome of the present war.

The developing crisis in Kurdistan does not bode well for the United States. It means that Washington is faced with accelerating destabilization throughout the *whole* Gulf region. In the south, Khomeini-style Islamic fundamentalism is actively trying to undermine the moderate Arab states, and in the Turkish-Iraq-Iran triangle there is now the prospect of widespread anarchy. On the basis of such scant information it is not useful to speculate further, but it does appear, as of January 1984, that the Kurdish question is once more pushing toward the front burner of international politics.

The Twelve-Point Program of 1966

In its desire to put an end to the unnatural conditions in certain parts of the north, according to paragraph four of the letter of designation forming a Government, to preserve the unity of Iraqi soil and to achieve national unity, to confirm the existing bonds between Arabs and Kurds—which require them to act sincerely and persistently in the interest of their common homeland—this Government announces the following program and declares its categorical determination to abide by it and to apply it in letter and spirit as soon as possible.

1. The Government has categorically recognized Kurdish nationality in the amended provisional constitution and is ready to emphasise and clarify this point in the permanent constitution, whereby Kurdish nationality and the national rights of the Kurds within the one Iraqi homeland, which includes two main nationalities—Arab and Kurdish—will become clear, and Arabs and Kurds will enjoy equal rights and duties.

2. The Government is ready to give this wholesome fact its real existence in the provincial law, which is to be promulgated on a decentralised basis. Each province, district and subdistrict will have a recognised corporate personality. Furthermore, each administrative unit will have its own elected council which will exercise wide powers in education, health,

Text taken from Majid Khadduri, *Republican Iraq* (London: Oxford University Press, 1969), pp. 274 ff.

and other local affairs, in addition to anything that has any connection with domestic and municipal affairs as detailed in the said law. The same law authorises amendments within the framework of administrative units. It also authorises the establishment of new administrative units when necessary according to the public interest.

3. Needless to say, the Government recognises the Kurdish language as an official language in addition to Arabic in regions where the majority of the population is Kurdish. Education will be in both languages in accordance with the limits defined by law and the local councils.

4. This Government intends to hold parliamentary elections within the period stipulated in the provisional constitution and the Cabinet policy statement. The Kurds will be represented in the next national council in a percentage proportionate to the whole population and according to the procedure laid down by the election law.

5. Also needless to say, the Kurds will share with their Arab brothers all public posts in proportion to their population, including ministries, public departments, and judicial, diplomatic and military posts, with due regard for the principle of efficiency.

6. There will be a number of scholarships, fellowships and study grants in all branches and at all levels for the Kurds, who are to be sent abroad for specialisation with due regard for efficiency and the country's needs. Baghdad University will give special attention to the study of the Kurdish language and its literature and its ideological and historical traditions. The University will open branches in the north when funds are available.

7. Needless to say, government officials in the Kurdish provinces, districts and subdistricts will be Kurds as long as the required number is available. Such posts will not be given to others unless it is in the interests of the region.

8. Parliamentary life will be accomplished by the establishment of certain political organisations. The press will be enabled to express the people's desire. The Government will

allow the Kurds to do so within the limits provided by law. The political and literary press in the Kurdish regions will be in the Kurdish or the Arabic language or in both languages according to the request of the people concerned.

9. (a) When acts of violence end, general amnesty will be granted to all those who participated in acts of violence in the north or who had any connection with them, including all those against whom sentences were issued in connection with such acts of violence, those related to them, and those whose freedoms have been suspended.

(b) All Kurdish officials and employees will return to their previous posts and employment will be treated with justice.

(c) The Government will do its best to return all dismissed Kurdish workers to their previous employment.

10. Immediately after issue of this statement, men of the armed forces will return to their units, provided all this takes place within two months. Those returning will be treated sympathetically and will be granted amnesty.

(a) Those who were in the army should return to the army with their arms.

(b) Those who were in the police force should return to the police force with their arms.

(c) Those who have borne arms will be regarded as a body attached to the Government, which will assist them to resume a normal life. Until this is done the Government will be responsible for them. All those who resume a normal life should surrender all their equipment, arms and ammunition to the Government. All this will be carried out by all concerned according to a prearranged plan.

(d) The *chevaliers* will naturally return to their positions when peace is established. Their arms will be withdrawn according to a prearranged plan.

11. Needless to say, funds now being spent resisting violence—funds spent unnecessarily—will be spent on the reconstruction of the north. A special organisation will be formed to reconstruct the Kurdish region in Iraq. The necessary money

will be allotted to it from the economic plan to undertake reconstruction and development projects in the area. The administration of summer resorts in the north and afforestation and tobacco affairs in the north will be assigned to a special Minister who will supervise the co-ordination of the affairs of the administrative units the majority of whose inhabitants are Kurds and whose affairs are at the heart of the Kurdish question—affairs such as Kurdish culture and education in the Kurdish language. The Government will do its best to compensate all those who suffered damage to enable them to return to a productive and useful life in security and peace and to participate in the promotion of the country's economy and prosperity. For national and humanitarian reasons the Government will take care of all orphans, widows and disabled who have been victims of violence in the northern part of the homeland. In co-operation with the department concerned the Government will establish shelter and professional institutions as soon as possible.

12. The Government will endeavor to resettle all individuals and groups who left or were evacuated from their regions with the aim of re-establishing a normal situation. Anything the Government finds necessary to control later in the general interest should, according to the provisions of the law be coupled with a speedy and fair compensation.

Notes

Chapter 1: Introduction

1. Dana Adams Schmidt, *Journey Among Brave Men* (Boston: Little, Brown and Co., 1964), pp. 8–9.

2. Gerard Chaliand, ed., *People Without a Country* (London: Zed Press, 1978), pp. 47, 108, 109, 154, 211, 220.

3. Derk Kinnane, *The Kurds and Kurdistan* (London: Oxford University Press, 1964), p. 2.

4. Sir Arnold Wilson suggests in *A Clash of Loyalties* (Oxford: Humphrey Milford, 1931) that when the Kurds murdered two British officers, the proper thing to have done would have been to evict the Kurds and give their land to the Assyrians.

5. Ibid., p. 127.

6. André Singer, "The Dervishes of Kurdistan," *Asian Affairs* 61:2 (June 1974), pp. 179–182.

7. Ely Bannister Soane, *To Mesopotamia and Kurdistan in Disguise* (Amsterdam: Amorica Book Co/Apa, 1979), p. 367.

8. Abdur Rahman Ghassemlou, *Kurdistan and the Kurds* (Prague: Publishing House of the Czechoslovak Academy of Science, 1965), p. 42.

9. The idea that what obtained in the Middle East during the period discussed here and in the next chapter was indeed feudalism is not at all widely accepted. Some Marxist writers, among others, reject this description. For example, Maxime Rodinson in *Islam and Capitalism* (Austin: University of Texas Press, 1978) says that there are too many profound differences between the two forms of feudalism to permit this neat correlation. Although recognizing that there are fundamental differences, I hold that the term is worth applying for want of a better one. For more about this

193

debate see Karl Marx, *Precapitalist Economic Formations* (New York: International Publishers, 1980), with an introduction by Eric Hobsbawm.

10. Fredrik Barth, *Principles of Social Organization in Southern Kurdistan* (Oslo: Brodrene Jorgensen A.S., 1953), p. 35.

11. Ismet Vanly, "Kurdistan in Iraq," in Chaliand, *People Without a Country,* p. 174.

12. Xenophon, *The Anabasis* (New York: Harper and Bros., 1847) pp. 84 ff.

13. V. Minorsky's article on the Kurds in the *Encyclopaedia of Islam* (Leiden: Brill, 1960), 2:1927; unless otherwise cited, all historical references in this section are from this article.

14. The words of the song "Pyshtmergayn" were translated for me by a Kurdish guerrilla; I assume they are accurate.

15. *Encyclopaedia Britannica* (New York: Encyclopaedia Britannica Co., 1911), s.v. "Kurds." ·

16. Hanna Batatu, *The Old Social Classes and the Revolutionary Movements of Iraq* (Princeton: Princeton University Press, 1978), pp. 37–38.

17. For the effect of bipolarity on stability see Kenneth Waltz, *Theory of International Politics* (New York: Addison-Wesley, 1979).

18. See Antonio Gramsci, "The State and Civil Society," in *Prison Notebooks* (New York: International Publishers, 1980), pp. 230 ff. Gramsci discusses the limitations of Kurdish-type movements (among others, he singles out the Bulgarian *comitadjis*) vis-à-vis mobilizing populations.

19. Archie Roosevelt, quoted in Ghassemlou, *Kurdistan and the Kurds,* p. 75, says: "It is one of the deadlocks of Kurdish nationalism that while not only its leaders but almost the entire rank and file should have their origin among the educated burghers, its military force always had to come from the tribes and their chiefs, who have neither the erudition nor other ideas but expectations of gaining profit and booty by impairing the government's authority."

20. My articles on Kurdistan for the *Milwaukee Journal* ran over two months, November–December 1964, under the title "Rendezvous with Rebels."

21. See Antonio Gramsci, "Modern Prince," in *Prison Notebooks,* p. 154, where he discusses the difficulty of determining the autonomy of a given movement and the silliness of assuming that

all movements must be autonomous. See also the same author's discussion (ibid., p. 178) of the difference between an organic and a conjunctural movement.

Chapter 2: Detribalization and Anarchy and Expansion

1. V. Lutsky, *Modern History of the Arab Countries* (Moscow: Progress Publishers, 1969), pp. 10 ff.

2. Ibid.

3. Claudius Rich, *Narrative of a Residence in Koordistan [sic]*, 2 vols. (London: James Duncan, 1836), 1:90.

4. Cf. Ivan the Terrible's treatment of the boyars in R. Skrynnikov, *Ivan the Terrible* (Gulf Breeze, Fla.: Academic International, 1981), pp. 22 ff.

5. Stephen Longrigg, *Four Centuries of Modern Iraq* (Oxford: Clarendon Press, 1925), p. 208.

6. Rich, *Narrative of a Residence,* p. 359.

7. Ibid., pp. 208 ff.

8. Longrigg, *Four Centuries,* pp. 208 ff.

9. Ibid.

10. Rich, *Narrative of a Residence,* p. 323.

11. C. J. Edmonds, *Kurds, Turks, and Arabs* (London: Oxford University Press, 1957), p. 55.

12. Longrigg, *Four Centuries,* p. 285.

13. Edmonds, *Kurds, Turks, and Arabs,* p. 55.

14. Lutsky, *Modern History,* pp. 24 ff.

15. *Encyclopaedia Britannica* (New York: Encyclopaedia Britannica Co., 1911), s.v. "Kurdistan."

16. Longrigg, *Four Centuries,* p. 285.

17. Ibid., p. 286.

18. Ibid.

19. V. Minorsky's article on the Kurds in the *Encyclopaedia of Islam* (Leiden: Brill, 1960), 2:1147.

20. The fate of Badr Khan contrasts sharply with that of Kor Mohammad. The Turks murdered the latter, but they, in effect, allowed Badr Khan to rusticate. Another figure, whom we will be looking at shortly, Shaikh Obaidullah, was similarly well treated by the Turks. Although supposedly a rebel against Turkish authority, the shaikh was captured and transported to Mecca where he died.

21. Longrigg, *Four Centuries,* p. 306.

22. Hanna Batatu, *The Old Social Classes and the Revolutionary Movements of Iraq* (Princeton: Princeton University Press, 1978), pp. 95 ff.

23. Zaki Salem, *Origins of British Influence in Mesopotamia* (New York: Columbia University Press, 1941), pp. 95 ff.

24. Longrigg, *Four Centuries,* p. 307.

25. Ibid., p. 285.

26. Batatu, *Old Social Classes,* p. 39.

27. Edmonds, *Kurds, Turks, and Arabs,* pp. 62 ff.

28. Ibid.

29. Ibid.

30. Ely Bannister Soane, *To Mesopotamia and Kurdistan in Disguise* (Amsterdam: Amorica Book Co/Apa, 1979), pp. 187ff.

31. Edmonds, *Kurds, Turks, and Arabs,* p. 30.

32. Soane, *To Mesopotamia and Kurdistan in Disguise,* pp. 187 ff.

33. Ibid., pp. 189ff.

34. Ibid., p. 190.

35. Batatu, *Old Social Classes,* p. 164.

36. Ibid., p. 59.

37. Sir Mark Sykes, *The Caliph's Last Heritage,* (London: Macmillan, 1915), p. 324.

38. Minorsky's article on the Kurds, 2:1148.

39. Longrigg, *Four Centuries,* p. 299.

40. Lutsky, *Modern History,* p. 324.

41. Sykes, *Caliph's Last Heritage,* p. 558.

42. Soane, *To Mesopotamia and Kurdistan in Disguise,* p. 189.

43. Sykes, *Caliph's Last Heritage,* pp. 317 ff.

44. Soane, *To Mesopotamia and Kurdistan in Disguise,* p. 189.

45. Edmonds, *Kurds, Turks, and Arabs,* p. 43.

46. Ibid.

47. *Encyclopaedia Britannica,* s.v. "Turkey," p. 463.

48. Ibid., "Armenia," p. 567.

49. Minorsky's article on the Kurds, 2:1148.

50. Cf. the article on "Armenia" (p. 568) with that on "Turkey" (p. 463) in the *Encyclopaedia Britannica.*

51. Ibid., "Kurdistan."

52. Arshak Safrastian, *The Kurds and Kurdistan* (London: Harvill Press, 1948), p. 50.

Chapter 3: The First Stirrings of Nationalism

1. Sir Arnold Wilson, *A Clash of Loyalties* (Oxford: Humphrey Milford, 1931), p. 31.
2. George Lenczowski, *Russia and the West in Iran* (Ithaca, N.Y.: Cornell University Press, 1949), p. 15.
3. Wilson, *Clash of Loyalties,* p. 32.
4. Hasan Arfa, *The Kurds* (London: Oxford University Press, 1966), pp. 48 ff.
5. Wilson, *Clash of Loyalties,* pp. 24 ff.
6. Ibid.
7. William Eagleton, Jr., *The Kurdish Republic of 1946* (London: Oxford University Press, 1963), p. 10.
8. Arshak Safrastian, *The Kurds and Kurdistan* (London: Harvill Press, 1948), p. 77.
9. Abdur Rahman Ghassemlou, *Kurdistan and the Kurds* (Prague: Publishing House of the Czechoslovak Academy of Science, 1965), p. 20.
10. C. J. Edmonds, *Kurds, Turks, and Arabs* (London: Oxford University Press, 1957), p. 398.
11. H.W.V. Temperley, *A History of the Peace Conference of Paris* (London: Oxford University Press, 1924), p. 192.
12. Ibid., p. 191.
13. Ibid.
14. Edmonds, *Kurds, Turks, and Arabs,* p. 29.
15. Wilson, *Clash of Loyalties,* p. 132.
16. Ibid., p. 113.
17. Ibid., pp. 336 ff.
18. Sir Arnold Toynbee, *Survey of International Affairs, 1925* (London: Humphrey Milford, Oxford University Press, 1927), p. 529.
19. Wilson, *Clash of Loyalties,* p. 268.
20. Ernest Main, *Iraq from Mandate to Independence* (London: Allen and Unwin, 1935), pp. 50 ff.
21. Edmonds, *Kurds, Turks, and Arabs,* pp. 68 ff.
22. Ibid., p. 124.
23. Ibid., p. 30.
24. Ibid., p. 123.
25. Ibid., p. 122.
26. Ibid., p. 339.
27. Ghassemlou, *Kurdistan and the Kurds,* p. 70.

28. Hasan Arfa, *Under Five Shahs* (New York: H. B. Morrow, 1965), p. 150.

29. Arfa, *The Kurds,* pp. 33 ff.

30. Sir Arnold Toynbee, *Turkey* (New York: Scribner, 1927), p. 265.

31. Arfa, *The Kurds,* p. 34.

32. Turkish troops had been sent to the rebel area along French-controlled rail lines in Syria (see Sir Arnold Toynbee, *Survey of International Affairs, 1928* [London: Humphrey Milford, Oxford University Press, 1929], p. 509).

33. Arfa, *The Kurds,* p. 37.

34. Ibid., p. 56.

35. Ibid., pp. 48 ff.

Chapter 4: The Nation States and the Reactionary Challenge

1. George Lenczowski, *Russia and the West in Iran* (Ithaca, N.Y.: Cornell University Press, 1949), p. 15.

2. Sir Arnold Toynbee, *Survey of International Affairs, 1928* (London: Humphrey Milford, Oxford University Press, 1929), p. 365.

3. Lenczowski, *Russia and the West in Iran,* p. 251.

4. Ernest Main, *Iraq from Mandate to Independence* (London: Allen and Unwin, 1935), p. 79.

5. Hasan Arfa, *Under Five Shahs* (New York: H. B. Morrow, 1965), p. 284.

6. Ibid., p. 170.

7. Ibid.

8. Ibid., p. 188.

9. Ibid., p. 218.

10. Lenczowski, *Russia and the West in Iran,* p. 74.

11. Gerard Chaliand, ed., *People Without a Country* (London: Zed Press, 1978), p. 114.

12. For example, Chaliand, *People Without a Country.*

13. Abdur Rahman Ghassemlou, *Kurdistan and the Kurds* (Prague: Publishing House of the Czechoslovak Academy of Science, 1965), p. 54.

14. Ibid., p. 53.

15. Chaliand, *People Without a Country,* p. 64.

16. Hasan Arfa, *The Kurds* (London: Oxford University Press, 1966), p. 39.

17. Ibid., p. 42.

18. Quoted in ibid., p. 68.

19. Quoted in Chaliand, *People Without a Country,* p. 27.

20. Ghassemlou, *Kurdistan and the Kurds,* pp. 59–60.

21. Arshak Safrastian, *The Kurds and Kurdistan* (London: Harvill Press, 1948), p. 85.

22. V. Minorsky's article on the Kurds in the *Encyclopaedia of Islam* (Leiden: Brill, 1960), 2:1149.

23. Arfa, *The Kurds,* p. 44.

24. Hanna Batatu, *The Old Social Classes and the Revolutionary Movements of Iraq* (Princeton: Princeton University Press, 1978), p. 82.

25. Ibid., p. 24.

26. Ibid., p. 47.

27. Ibid., p. 49.

28. Ibid., p. 102.

29. Ibid., p. 95.

30. Ibid., p. 104.

31. Ibid., p. 82.

32. Ibid., p. 98.

33. Ibid., p. 96.

34. Ibid., pp. 77–78.

35. Ibid., p. 110.

36. Sir Arnold Toynbee, *Survey of International Affairs, 1934* (London: Humphrey Milford, Oxford University Press, 1935), p. 118.

37. Ibid., pp. 135 ff.

38. Main, *Iraq from Mandate to Independence,* pp. 145 ff.

39. Toynbee, *Survey of International Affairs, 1934,* p. 166.

40. Ibid., p. 152.

41. Ibid., p. 153.

42. Toynbee, *Survey of International Affairs, 1928,* p. 366.

43. Chaliand, *People Without a Country,* p. 163.

Chapter 5: The Kurdish Republic and Russian Involvement

1. William Eagleton, Jr., *The Kurdish Republic of 1946* (London: Oxford University Press, 1963), p. 91.

2. For a discussion of defensive and aggressive nationalism see Bronislaw Malinowski, "An Anthropological Analysis of War," *American Journal of Sociology* 46 (1941), pp. 521–550.

3. Fredrik Barth, *Principles of Social Organization in Southern Kurdistan* (Oslo: Brodrene Jorgensen A.S., 1953).

4. C. J. Edmonds, "The Kurds and the Revolution in Iraq," *Middle East Journal* 13 (1959), p. 5.

5. Eagleton, *Kurdish Republic of 1946,* p. 47.

6. Sir Mark Sykes, *The Caliph's Last Heritage,* (London: Macmillan, 1915), p. 433.

7. Eagleton, *Kurdish Republic of 1946,* p. 48.

8. C. J. Edmonds, *Kurds, Turks, and Arabs* (London: Oxford University Press, 1957), pp. 62 ff.

9. Edmonds, "The Kurds and the Revolution in Iraq," p. 5.

10. Hasan Arfa, *The Kurds* (London: Oxford University Press, 1966), p. 118.

11. Eagleton, *Kurdish Republic of 1946,* p. 51.

12. Hanna Batatu, *The Old Social Classes and the Revolutionary Movements of Iraq* (Princeton: Princeton University Press, 1978), p. 662.

13. Eagleton, *Kurdish Republic of 1946,* p. 51.

14. Arfa, *The Kurds,* p. 119.

15. Edmonds, "The Kurds and the Revolution in Iraq," p. 6.

16. Arfa, *The Kurds,* p. 119; see also Edgar O'Ballance, *The Kurdish Revolt 1961–70* (London: Archon Books, 1973), p. 44.

17. Dana Adams Schmidt, *Journey Among Brave Men* (Boston: Little, Brown and Co., 1964), p. 100.

18. Eagleton, *Kurdish Republic of 1946,* pp. 55–56.

19. George Lenczowski, *Russia and the West in Iran* (Ithaca, N.Y.: Cornell University Press, 1949), p. 249.

20. Ibid., p. 112.

21. Ibid.

22. Hasan Arfa, *Under Five Shahs* (New York: W. B. Morrow, 1965), pp. 350–351.

23. Ibid.

24. Eagleton, *Kurdish Republic of 1946,* p. 27; also Arfa, *The Kurds,* p. 93.

25. Eagleton, *Kurdish Republic of 1946,* p. 73.

26. Arfa, *Under Five Shahs,* p. 324.

27. Eagleton, *Kurdish Republic of 1946,* p. 324.

28. Ibid., pp. 32 ff.

29. Ibid.

30. Ibid., p. 36.

31. Arfa, *The Kurds,* p. 77.
32. Eagleton, *Kurdish Republic of 1946,* p. 30.
33. Ibid., p. 39.
34. O'Ballance, *Kurdish Revolt,* p. 49.
35. Eagleton, *Kurdish Republic of 1946,* p. 43.
36. Ibid., p. 44.
37. Ibid., p. 45.
38. Ibid., p. 55.
39. Ibid., p. 62.
40. Ibid., Plate 16.
41. Ibid., p. 67.
42. Arfa, *Under Five Shahs,* p. 348.
43. Archie Roosevelt, Jr., "The Kurdish Republic of Mahabad," *Middle East Journal* 1 (July 1947), p. 264.
44. Eagleton, *Kurdish Republic of 1946,* pp. 87 ff.
45. Ibid., p. 100.
46. Ibid., p. 87.
47. Ibid., p. 100.
48. Ibid., p. 87.
49. Ibid.
50. Ibid., p. 92.
51. Abdur Rahman Ghassemlou, "Kurdistan in Iran," in Gerard Chaliand, ed., *People Without a Country* (London: Zed Press, 1978), p. 119.
52. Eagleton, *Kurdish Republic of 1946,* p. 102.
53. Ibid., pp. 77–78.
54. Ibid.
55. Ibid.
56. O'Ballance, *Kurdish Revolt,* pp. 36–37.
57. Sir Mark Sykes, *Dar ul Islam* (London: Bickers and Son, 1904), p. 207.
58. Eagleton, *Kurdish Republic of 1946,* pp. 49 ff.
59. W. R. Hay, *Two Years in Kurdistan* (London: Sidgewick and Jackson, 1921), p. 371.
60. O'Ballance, *Kurdish Revolt,* p. 51.
61. Eagleton, *Kurdish Republic of 1946,* pp. 85–86.
62. Ibid., p. 82.
63. Arfa, *The Kurds,* p. 95.
64. Eagleton, *Kurdish Republic of 1946,* p. 106.
65. Arfa, *The Kurds,* p. 94.

66. Eagleton, *Kurdish Republic of 1946,* p. 107.
67. Ibid., p. 112.
68. Ibid., pp. 112–113.
69. Ibid., pp. 121 ff.
70. Ibid., p. 125.
71. Ibid., pp. 116 ff.
72. Ibid., p. 126.

Chapter 6: The Nationalist Movement in Crisis

1. Lorenzo Kimball, *Changing Pattern of Political Power in Iraq* (New York: Robert Speller, 1972), p. 89.
2. Uriel Dann, *Iraq Under Qassem* (New York: Praeger, 1969), p. 109.
3. Caractacus [pseud.], *Revolution in Iraq* (London: Gollancz, 1959), p. 109.
4. Dana Adams Schmidt, *Journey Among Brave Men* (Boston: Little, Brown and Co., 1964), p. 104.
5. Dann, *Iraq Under Qassem,* p. 98.
6. Hanna Batatu, *The Old Social Classes and the Revolutionary Movements of Iraq* (Princeton: Princeton University Press, 1978), p. 699.
7. Caractacus, *Revolution in Iraq,* p. 149.
8. Majid Khadduri, *Republican Iraq* (London: Oxford University Press, 1969), p. 149.
9. Conversation with the author.
10. Khadduri, *Republican Iraq,* p. 152.
11. Ibid., p. 110.
12. Ibid.
13. George Lenczowski, *Russia and the West in Iran* (Ithaca, N.Y.: Cornell University Press, 1949), p. 293.
14. Ibid.
15. Batatu, *Old Social Classes,* pp. 912 ff.
16. Schmidt, *Journey Among Brave Men,* pp. 92 ff.
17. Ibid.
18. Ibid. -
19. Ibid., p. 113.
20. Ibid., p. 114.
21. Hasan Arfa, *The Kurds* (London: Oxford University Press, 1966), p. 130.

22. Edgar O'Ballance, *The Kurdish Revolt 1961–70* (London: Archon Books, 1973), p. 64.

23. Ibid.

24. Conversations with the author.

25. O'Ballance, *Kurdish Revolt,* p. 71.

26. Arfa, *The Kurds,* p. 133.

27. Dann, *Iraq Under Qassem,* p. 334.

28. Arfa, *The Kurds,* p. 134.

29. Dann, *Iraq Under Qassem,* p. 136.

30. Arfa, *The Kurds,* p. 135.

31. O'Ballance, *Kurdish Revolt,* p. 48.

32. Schmidt, *Journey Among Brave Men,* p. 128.

33. Dann, *Iraq Under Qassem,* p. 375.

34. Ibid.

35. Schmidt, *Journey Among Brave Men,* p. 72.

36. O'Ballance, *Kurdish Revolt,* p. 68.

37. Dann, *Iraq Under Qassem,* p. 333.

38. Schmidt, *Journey Among Brave Men,* p. 72.

39. Dann, *Iraq Under Qassem,* p. 336.

40. Ibid.

41. O'Ballance, *Kurdish Revolt,* p. 88.

42. Ibid., p. 77.

43. Dann, *Iraq Under Qassem,* p. 341.

44. O'Ballance, *Kurdish Revolt,* p. 78.

45. Ibid., p. 88.

46. Dann, *Iraq Under Qassem,* p. 341.

47. O'Ballance, *Kurdish Revolt,* p. 78.

48. Ibid.

49. Ibid.

50. Ibid., p. 79.

51. Schmidt, *Journey Among Brave Men,* p. 80.

52. Ibid.

53. Ibid., p. 84.

54. O'Ballance, *Kurdish Revolt,* p. 96.

55. Ibid., pp. 95 ff.

56. Ibid., p. 96.

57. Schmidt, *Journey Among Brave Men,* p. 255.

58. Ibid., p. 258.

59. Sir Arnold Toynbee, *Survey of International Affairs, 1963* (London: Oxford University Press, 1977), pp. 193 ff.

60. Ibid.

61. Derk Kinnane, *The Kurds and Kurdistan* (London: Oxford University Press, 1964), p. 75.

62. Abdur Rahman Ghassemlou, *Kurdistan and the Kurds* (Prague: Publishing House of the Czechoslovak Academy of Science, 1965), p. 75.

63. Arfa, *The Kurds,* p. 146.

64. Khadduri, *Republican Iraq,* p. 203.

65. Telebani in a conversation with the author.

66. See Appendix.

Chapter 7: An Assessment of the Crisis

1. Dana Adams Schmidt, *Journey Among Brave Men* (Boston: Little, Brown and Co., 1964), p. 285.

2. Quotations from Ahmad, Telebani, Shamzini, and Barzani are all, unless otherwise noted, taken from interviews I conducted in Iran and Iraq in 1964.

3. Schmidt, *Journey Among Brave Men,* p. 285.

4. Chris Kutschera, *Le Mouvement National Kurde* (Paris: Flammarion, 1979), pp. 244 ff.

5. An Iranian officer described Barzani to me as being "tres politique." Barzani is the fox, he said, who eats the chickens. Ahmad said of him, "He's ambiguous. You will see when you interview him."

6. The Kurdish-Iraqi negotiations over how much autonomy the Kurds could expect were strikingly like the haggling between the Israelis and the Egyptians over similar concessions to the Palestinians. The difficulty in agreeing seems to have arisen over the fact that any genuine grant of autonomy leads inevitably to secession.

7. Ahmad said Yahia's protestations over the agreement were a sham. The KDP made many more radical demands than this.

8. Ahmad was the actual leader of the Barzani tribe, a position he held by right of his religious status—a shaikh of the Naqshbandi sect.

9. As told to me in his headquarters at Raniyah some days after I had interviewed Ahmad and Telebani in Iran.

10. A particular scourge was malaria. The people being poor and hospitals nonexistent, the disease tended to develop into cerebral malaria. Mostly children died of it. The desperate need was for

chloroquine, which the government allegedly refused to supply, claiming the Kurds restricted its use to the *pysht merga* (Kurdish guerrillas).

11. A clear threat of a Communist takeover of the movement.

12. Meaning there are 110 million Arabs in the Middle East who do not warrant antagonizing. This, supposedly, was the same consideration that induced the Russians to pull back on their plan to have Outer Mongolia bring up the question of Iraqi genocide against the Kurds in the United Nations.

13. Specifically, as-Sulaymaniyah, Irbil, Kirkuk, and the Kurdish areas of Mosel. The government had conceded Dohuk, Zakho, Amadia, Shaikhan and Akka—all in the far north. Kirkuk, the major oil area, was the main sticking point.

14. *New York Times,* August 2, 1963.

15. Ibid., July 6, 1963.

16. Not much is known definitely about the degree of support actually tendered to the Kurds by the Israelis. The Kurds, while acknowledging that support was forthcoming, refused to specify details as long as they entertained a hope of reconciliation with the Arabs.

Chapter 8: The Continuing Kurdish Question

1. For example, William Safire, *New York Times,* February 5 and 12, 1976.

2. The House Select Committee on Intelligence published a report (the Pike Report) on investigations of CIA covert operations involving the Kurds. An alleged copy of the report was leaked to the *Village Voice,* which printed it beginning February 23, 1976.

3. *New York Times,* July 28, 1968.

4. Ibid., January 19, 1969.

5. Ibid.

6. Ibid., January 28, 1969.

7. Subsequent revelations of Israeli Prime Minister Begin throw further light on the allegations.

8. Edgar O'Ballance, *The Kurdish Revolt 1961–70* (London: Archon Books, 1973), pp. 151 ff,

9. *New York Times,* April 26, 1970.

10. Ibid., June 3, 1972.

11. Martin Short and Anthony McDermutt, *The Kurds* (London: Minority Rights Group, 1975).

12. *New York Times,* April 6, 1975.

13. Ibid., September 29, 1974.

14. *Village Voice,* February 23, 1976.

15. Ibid., February 26, 1976.

16. *New York Times,* February 4, 1974.

17. Ismet Vanly, "Kurdistan in Iraq," in Gerard Chaliand, ed., *People Without a Country* (London: Zed Press, 1978), p. 171.

18. *New York Times,* February 4, 1975.

19. Ibid., April 13, 1974.

20. Quoted in Chaliand, *People Without a Country,* p. 181.

21. *Village Voice,* February 26, 1976.

22. Ibid.

23. Ibid.

24. Ibid.

25. Ibid.

26. For example, the 1971 assassination of Defense Minister Hardan Takriti in Kuwait.

27. *New York Times,* April 1, 1976.

28. Ibid., March 19, 1975.

29. Ibid., March 13, 1970; italics mine.

30. Vanly, "Kurdistan in Iraq," pp. 182–192.

31. Ibid., p. 191.

32. *New York Times,* April 1, 1974.

33. David G. Adams, author of *Kurdish War* (London: Allen and Unwin, 1964), in a letter to the author.

34. Vanly, "Kurdistan in Iraq," p. 191.

35. Ibid.

36. Ibid.

37. *New York Times,* April 6, 1976.

38. Vanly, "Kurdistan in Iraq," p. 187.

39. Ibid., p. 189.

40. Short and McDermutt, *The Kurds,* p. 21.

41. Chaliand, *People Without a Country,* pp. 196, 201.

42. *New York Times,* March 1, 1979.

43. Ibid., March 20, 1979.

44. Ibid., May 31, 1980.

45. Ibid., May 1, 1979.

46. Ibid., October 11, 1979.

47. Ibid., October 14, 1979.
48. Ibid., May 31, 1980.
49. Ibid., March 16, 1981.
50. *Christian Science Monitor,* January 28, 1981.
51. *New York Times,* April 9, 1981.
52. *Christian Science Monitor,* May 9, 1981.

Index